ESSENTIAL MESSAGES FROM GOD'S SERVANTS

masterWork®

Lessons from

AUTHENTIC CHRISTIANITY

by Ray C. Stedman

WHEN GODLY PEOPLE DO UNGODLY THINGS

by Beth Moore

SUMMER *2007*

Send questions/comments to
Editor, *MasterWork*
One LifeWay Plaza
Nashville, TN 37234-0175
Or make comments on the web at
www.lifeway.com

ACKNOWLEDGMENTS.–We believe the Bible has God for its author; salvation for its end; and truth, without any mixture of error, for its matter and that all Scripture is totally true and trustworthy. The 2000 statement of *The Baptist Faith and Message* is our doctrinal guideline.

MasterWork: Essential Messages from God's Servants (ISSN 1542-703X) is published quarterly by LifeWay Christian Resources of the Southern Baptist Convention, One LifeWay Plaza, Nashville, Tennessee 37234; Thom Rainer, President. Single subscription to individual address, $26.35 per year. If you need help with an order, WRITE LifeWay Church Resources Customer Service, One LifeWay Plaza, Nashville, Tennessee 37234-0113; For subscriptions, FAX (615) 251-5818 or EMAIL *subscribe@lifeway.com.* For bulk shipments mailed quarterly to one address, FAX (615) 251-5933 or EMAIL *CustomerService@lifeway.com.* Order ONLINE at *www.lifeway.com.* Mail address changes to: *MasterWork*, One LifeWay Plaza, Nashville, TN 37234-0113.

Printed in the United States of America.

Cover photo credit:
© AbleStock.com/Jupiterimages Unlimited

table of Contents

master*Work*:
Essential Messages from God's Servants

- Designed for developing and maturing believers who desire to go deeper into the spiritual truths of God's Word.
- Ideal for many types of Bible study groups.
- A continuing series from leading Christian authors and their key messages.
- Based on LifeWay's well-known, interactive model for daily Bible study.
- The interspersed interactive personal learning activities **in bold type** are written by the writer identified on the Study Theme unit page.
- Teaching plans follow each lesson to help facilitators guide learners through lessons.
- Published quarterly.

ABOUT THE WRITERS

Ray C. Stedman

was one of the great Bible teachers of the 20th century. Ray's primary teaching method was expository preaching, systematically teaching through entire books of the Bible.

From 1948-1990 Ray was one of the key leaders at Peninsula Bible Church and the explosive growth of that church during that time was largely due to the power of Ray's teaching.

Although Ray went home to the Lord in 1992, his messages continue to have world wide impact as thousands of people use his materials available from Discovery House Publishers.

JOE BECKLER wrote the personal learning activities and teaching plans for this study. Joe holds a Master of Divinity degree from New Orleans Baptist Theological Seminary. Currently he is planting a church in Durango, Colorado. He enjoys participating in outdoor sports. Joe and Cheri also parent triplet sons.

ABOUT THIS STUDY

What is your initial reaction to the phrase "authentic Christianity"?

____

How would you define this phrase to someone who is unacquainted with the Christian faith?

____

Who in your life comes to mind as a good example of an authentic Christian?

____

Authentic Christianity

In these lessons we will explore a major passage from Paul's epistles—2 Corinthians 2:14 to 6:13. In this passage Paul helped the Corinthians distinguish between authentic Christianity, as he himself lived it, and the pale imitation that many of them had mistaken for the real thing.

The Apostle Paul patterned his life after the example of Christ (1 Cor. 11:1). As we examine this selection from Paul's second letter to the Christians at Corinth—one of the most biographical of all Paul's letters—we will gain insight into Paul's own experiences as an imitator of Christ and of His ministry. Here, Paul revealed to us in the clearest terms the secret of his own great ministry.

Ray C. Stedman

Unmistakable Marks of Authentic Christianity

Mark # 1: Unquenchable Optimism

The first one and one-half chapters of 2 Corinthians indicate that Paul was being challenged by certain Christians at Corinth. They had been affected by some Jewish Christians from Jerusalem who suggested that Paul was not a genuine apostle at all because (1) he was not one of the original twelve, and (2) some of his teachings went beyond the law of Moses. Claiming he was not a real apostle, they insisted his brand of Christianity was not real Christianity. One of the Devil's favorite tricks is to brand the truth as a big lie, and that's exactly what was happening at Corinth.

Paul's response to these charges is to describe for us the nature of his ministry. As we shall see, Paul's ministry bears five unmistakable qualities of Christianity that cannot be successfully counterfeited. These qualities have nothing to do with personality or temperament, so anyone who discovers the secret of authentic Christianity can attain them. They are timeless, so they are just as genuine in the twenty-first century as in the first.

Which best describes you, "Murphy's law" or belief in God's grace, love, and ultimate control?

____

In 2 Corinthians 2:14 we find the first three marks of authentic Christianity.

The first mark is found in the very first phrase: "Thanks be to God." One unmistakable evidence of radical Christianity is a spirit of thankfulness, even amid trial and difficulty. It is a kind of *unquenchable optimism.* The world operates by the gloomy principle of Murphy's Law: Whatever can go wrong, will go wrong. Authentic Christians operate by a belief in God's grace, love, and ultimate control.

What specifically about your life makes you feel the way you do?

____

This attitude of thanksgiving is genuine and profound. There is nothing artificial about it. It is a far cry from the imitation thanksgiving often seen in Christians today. Some people think they are expected to repeat pious and thankful words, even when they don't feel thankful. They assume that's the way Christians are supposed to act. Many have settled for a grin-and-bear-it attitude that even a non-Christian can adopt when there's nothing much he can do about a situation. But that is a long way from true Christian thankfulness. To listen to some Christians today, you would think God expects us to screw on a smile and go around saying, "Hallelujah, I've got cancer!" That's not what our unquenchable optimism is all about.

Authentic Christianity is rooted in reality. It feels all the hurt and pain of adverse circumstances and does not find any pleasure in them. But authentic Christianity does see the result being produced—not only in heaven, someday, but right now, here on earth. That result is so desirable and glorious, it is worth all the pain and heartache. That is why it can do nothing but rejoice! An authentic Christian is confident that the same Lord who permitted the pain to come will use it to bring about a highly desirable end. That is why we can be genuinely thankful—even in the midst of perplexity and sorrow.

"About midnight Paul and Silas were praying and singing hymns to God, and the other prisoners were listening to them" (Acts 16:25).

What catches your attention regarding Paul and Silas in the Acts 16 story? (Read Acts 16:16-40 for a full review of this amazing story.)

______

How do you react to the idea that God will take our pain and bring about a "highly desirable end"? ______

If possible, describe in the margin an example or an experience from your life to support your reaction.

How does Paul and Silas's reaction in Acts 16 relate to your own worst-case scenarios?

______

______

An outstanding example of this unquenchable optimism of authentic Christianity is in Acts 16. There, Paul and Silas find themselves at midnight in an inner dungeon in the city jail of Philippi. Their backs are raw and bloody from a terrible flogging received at the hands of the Roman authorities. Their feet are fastened in stocks. The future is uncertain and frightening. Anything could happen to them in the morning—even torture and death. There is no one around to be impressed by a show of courage, and no one to intervene and rescue them. Yet, despite all these reasons for pessimism and hopelessness, *Paul and Silas literally break into song!*

How would your typical reaction compare to theirs?

______

______

No one could accuse them of being phony or of putting up a good front just to keep up their spirits. They were genuinely thankful to God. They began to praise Him at midnight because they knew that, despite the apparent rebuff and lack of success, their objective had been accomplished. How could they have known what God had planned for them—an earthquake that would jar their chains loose, topple their prison walls, and set them free? They couldn't! They had no premonition at all of being set free. They were simply manifesting marks of authentic Christianity—unquenchable optimism and thanksgiving.

Where in your life, right now, is unquenchable optimism most needed? ____________________

Mark # 2: Unvarying Success

The second mark of authentic Christianity is closely linked to the first. It is found in the next phrase in 2 Corinthians 2:14, "who always leads us in triumphal procession in Christ." Note how strongly Paul puts it: Jesus "*always* leads us" in triumph. Not occasionally. Not sometimes. *Always.* The apostle makes perfectly clear that the Christianity he has experienced presents a pattern of *unvarying success.* It never involves failure but invariably achieves its goals. It involves, as we have seen, struggles and hardships and tears. Sometimes, as on the cross at Calvary, the moment of triumph may even look like complete failure. But our triumph is always assured. Though the struggle may be desperate, it is never serious. It issues at last in the complete achievement of the objectives God has set for us. Even the opposition we encounter is made to serve the purposes of victory.

We must remember that these high-sounding words of Paul's were written by a man who bore on his body the wounds of a servant of Jesus. He had endured much difficulty, endless disappointments, and bitter persecution with great pain. Yet he could write with rugged truthfulness that Jesus *always* leads us in triumph.

This certainly does not mean that Paul's plans and goals were always realized, for they were not. He wanted to do many things he was never able to accomplish. It is not Paul's plans that are in view here, but God's. The triumph is Christ's, not Paul's.

The invariable mark of authentic Christianity is that, once we have discovered its radical secret, we can never fail. Our will, our dreams, our goals, our desires may be thwarted—but God's will and plan? Never! He can even weave our apparent failures into His overall design for ultimate triumph. In the life of an authentic Christian, every obstacle becomes an opportunity. Success is inevitable.

Spiritually speaking, do you typically feel like you are on the "winning team"? Why or why not?

____

The unquenchable optimism of genuine Christianity shines through the first chapter of Paul's letter to his friends at Philippi. Writing as a prisoner in the city of Rome, confined to a private, rented home but chained day and night to a member of Caesar's imperial guard, Paul faces a very bleak future. He must soon appear before Nero Caesar to answer Jewish charges that could result in his death. He is no longer allowed to travel freely about the empire preaching. He cannot even visit his beloved friends.

When obstacles emerge, what is your attitude like?

____

What a time for discouragement! Yet no New Testament letter reflects greater confidence and rejoicing than Paul's letter to the Philippians. The reason for this confidence, Paul says, is twofold. He writes, "Now I want you to know, brothers, that what has happened to me has really served to advance the gospel" (Phil. 1:12). Then he lists two evidences to prove his point.

First, he says, "As a result, it has become clear throughout the whole palace guard and to everyone else that I am in chains for Christ" (Phil. 1:13). The palace guard (or, in some translations, the praetorian guard) is the imperial bodyguard. Since he is a prisoner of Caesar's, he must be guarded by Caesar's own hand-picked guard. The guard was largely made up of sons of noble families who were commissioned to spend a few years in Nero's palace guard. Later on, this select group would become the king-makers of the empire, responsible for choosing succeeding emperors. They were impressive young men, the cream of the empire, in training for future positions of power and leadership. Every six hours one of the future leaders of the Roman Empire was brought in, chained to Paul, and forcibly exposed to the life-changing gospel of Jesus Christ!

Paul took a negative dilemma and interpreted it as purposeful in Christ's plan. Identify and describe a situation where you have experienced a dilemma that turned out to have a positive, purposeful effect.

____

____

____

Second, as a result, some of these young men were being won to Christ. If you doubt that this was happening, just look at the next to the last verse of the Philippian letter: "All the saints send you greetings, especially those who belong to Caesar's household" (Phil. 4:22). Here is a band of young men, the political center of the empire, being infiltrated and conquered for Christ by an old man in chains awaiting trial for his life.

What circumstances surrounding Paul's situation could have led him to miss an opportunity to reach out to the young soldiers? (Review Phil. 1:12-30.) ________

____

How often do you feel like spiritual triumph is missed in your life simply because you wallowed in your unfortunate circumstances? ________________

____

"Because of my chains, most of the brothers in the Lord have been encouraged to speak the word of God more courageously and fearlessly" (Phil. 1:14).

Based on Paul's perspective and experience described in Philippians 1, what do you think you miss when you wallow in your own unfortunate circumstances?

____

____

In light of Philippians 1:14, fill in the blanks:

Because of ________, the following has happened ________

____

____

____

________________.

This incident is a magnificent revelation of God's strategy—and, by contrast, of the weakness of human strategy. No human mind could have conceived this unique approach to the very heart of the empire. We humans are forever planning strategies for fulfilling the Great Commission, but what we come up with is usually banal, routine, unimaginative, and relatively ineffective. The noteworthy thing about God's strategy is that it is ingenious and totally unexpected.

Paul makes a second point in his letter to the Philippians to support his claim that the things that happened to him had only served to advance the gospel. He says, "*Because of my chains,* most of the brothers in the Lord have been encouraged to speak the word of God more courageously and fearlessly" (Phil. 1:14, emphasis added). *Because Paul was a prisoner,* the Roman Christians were witnessing far more freely throughout the city than they would have done otherwise.

Mark # 3: Unforgettable Impact

The third unmistakable mark follows immediately. After saying, "Thanks be to God, who always leads us in triumphal procession in Christ," Paul continues with this beautiful statement of the impact we have as authentic Christians: "and through us spreads everywhere *the fragrance of the knowledge of him*" (2 Cor. 2:14, emphasis added). God tells us that our lives should be spent giving off a fragrance, a perfume, a pleasing bouquet—not only to other people but to God. Enlarging on this thought, Paul adds: "For we are to God the aroma of Christ among those who are being saved and those who are perishing. To the one we are the smell of death; to the other, the fragrance of life. And who is equal to such a task?" (vv. 15–16).

Describe what you think a Christian who embodies the aroma of Christ looks and acts like. ________________

____

Would people say that you carry such an aroma? ____

Why or why not? ____________________

____

Most men have had the experience of being in a room when a strikingly beautiful woman enters. Before she came in, she applied a touch here and there of fragrant perfume, and as she passes through the room, she leaves behind a lingering fragrance. Consciously or unconsciously, all the males in the room are affected by that fragrance. Weeks or months later, they may catch a wisp of that fragrance again—and immediately, the image of that beautiful woman flashes into their minds. The fragrance has made her unforgettable.

What is one unforgettable impression that Christianity has made on you?

Describe someone you know who has had a "life to life" reaction when presented with the aroma of Christ.

How would you describe the way Jesus is received in today's context?

What is your usual reaction if people have an adverse or antagonistic response to your faith?

How should you think, feel, and respond if someone hates you because of your faith in Jesus?

That is the picture Paul gives here. Authentic Christianity leaves an *unforgettable impression* on those who encounter it. Christians are responsible for the enduring impact they make. As Paul suggests, the impact may be in one of two directions. Christians either increase opposition to Christ (death to death) or they lead toward faith and life (life to life). If your life is one that reflects radical, authentic Christianity, people become either bitter or better through contact with you. But one thing cannot happen—people will never remain the same. Those who are determined to die are pushed on toward death by coming into contact with authentic Christianity. Those who are seeking to live are helped on into life. Jesus certainly had this quality about Him. No one ever came into contact with Him and went away the same.

Many commentators think Paul had in mind a typical Roman triumph when a Roman general returned to the capital after a successful campaign. A great procession passed through the streets of Rome displaying the captives who were taken in the course of the conquest. The prisoners who were destined to live and return to their captured country to govern it under Roman rule went before the chariot of the conqueror, bearing garlands of flowers and pots of fragrant incense. Other prisoners followed behind the chariot dragging chains and heavy manacles. These were doomed to execution, for the Romans felt they could not trust them. As the procession went on through the cheering crowds, the incense pots and fragrant flowers were to the first group a fragrance from life to life while the same aroma was to the second group a fragrance of death to death.

This is the effect of the gospel as it touches the world through the life of an authentic Christian. Authentic Christianity leaves a lingering fragrance to God of Jesus Christ, no matter what—but to human beings, it is either a fragrance of death to death or of life to life.

But what about phony Christianity? That's another matter altogether—it's just a bad smell!

Mark # 4: Unimpeachable Integrity

The fourth mark of genuine Christianity is found in 2 Corinthians 2:17: "Unlike so many, we do not peddle the word of God for profit. On the contrary, in Christ we speak before God with sincerity, like men sent from God." Remember, that is primarily a reference to common, ordinary Christians who have learned the secret of authentic Christianity, not just to pastors.

Christians can be described in two ways, negatively and positively. Negatively, they are not peddlers, hucksters, or street salesmen. Much Christian preaching and witnessing can be described that way. People select certain attractive features from the Scriptures and use these as "selling points."

Is it OK to talk about your faith in terms of selling points? Explain.

Four Qualities of Integrity

Our integrity as authentic Christians is characterized by four qualities, according to this passage. First quality: We speak "with sincerity." In other words, we are to be honest people. We must mean what we say. The world admires sincerity and feels it is the ultimate expression of character—but according to Paul, sincerity is just the beginning of character, God's minimum expectation of authentic Christians. The very least we should expect from ourselves as Christians is that we thoroughly believe and practice what we say.

On a scale of 1 to 10 (1 being "very hard" and 10 being "extremely easy"), how easy or hard is it to "thoroughly believe and practice" your faith? ______

Why did you rate yourself this way?

____

Second quality: Paul says we are "sent from God." This speaks of our *purpose* as authentic Christians. The words can be rendered "commissioned by God" (RSV). We are not to be idle dreamers with no definite objective in view. We have been commissioned as military officers are commissioned. We have been given a definite task and specific assignments that constitute our purpose in life and in ministry. We are purposeful people with an end in view, an object to attain, a goal to accomplish,

How would you define your "definite task" and "specific assignment"? ____________

and we do not merely preach or witness as though that were a goal in itself.

Third quality: Paul says we do all this "before God" (or "in the sight of God," RSV). This indicates an attitude of transparency, of openness to investigation. To walk in the sight of other people permits us to hide our sins and contradictions behind a facade. But to walk in the sight of God requires total honesty with Him and with ourselves because nothing can be hidden from God's sight. There must be no cover-up or evasion of the facts of our sin when it occurs. There are no areas of denial. All is evaluated and tested by the purity and knowledge and wisdom of God—and what is sinful, we confess and we repent of before God. A man who walks in the sight of God is more interested in his inner reality than his outer reputation. He or she can be completely trusted.

Is this a hard exercise for you? Why or why not? ____________

What helps you remember that you live your life "before God"? ____________

Fourth quality: We speak "in Christ." What quality does that indicate? *Authority!* Paul states it clearly in 2 Corinthians 5:20—"We are therefore Christ's ambassadors, as though God were making his appeal through us." Ambassadors are authorized spokesmen. They have power to act and make covenants on behalf of others. Authentic Christians are not powerless servants. We speak words and deliver messages that heaven honors.

When are you most aware of God's presence? ____________

When are you typically least aware of God's presence? ____________

All of these qualities add up to *unimpeachable integrity.* People of sincerity, purpose, transparency, and authority are utterly trustworthy. Their word is their bond, and they can be counted on to come through. They are responsible and faithful individuals. That is the fourth great mark of real Christianity.

How does it feel to be an "authorized spokesman" on behalf of Christ? ____________

Of the four categories listed above, which is the strongest in your life? ____________

Which would be an area for growth? ____________

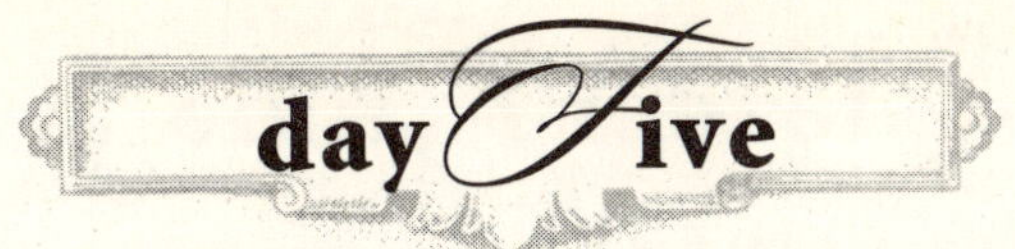

Mark # 5: Undeniable Reality

At this point in the Scripture we come to a chapter division. This is unfortunate because it divides two chapters that belong together. It's best to ignore the division and read on to find the fifth mark of authentic Christianity.

Paul is aware he is beginning to sound arrogant. Indeed, it is obvious from his words in 3:1–3 that some had even suggested in previous correspondence that the next time he came to Corinth he bring letters of recommendation from some of the Twelve in Jerusalem! But Paul says to them in effect, "You want letters of recommendation to prove I have authority as a messenger of God? Why, you yourselves are all the recommendation I need! Look what has happened to you. Are you any different since you came to Christ through my word? Your own hearts will bear witness to yourselves and before the world that the message you heard from us and which has changed your lives is from God."

Are you any different since you came to Christ? _____

Read 1 Corinthians 6:9–11 printed in the margin. Here is the final mark of genuine Christianity: undeniable reality, a change that cannot be explained on any other terms than God at work.

If someone asked you to prove that God changed your life, what would you say? ____________________

These are the five unmistakable signs of genuine Christianity. But the truly remarkable thing is that becoming a Christian does not of itself guarantee that these Christian graces will be manifest in us. It is not *being* a Christian that produces these, but *living* as a Christian. There is a knowledge we must have and a choice we must make before these virtues will be consistently present. The secret awaits us in the next lesson.

"Are we beginning to commend ourselves again? Or do we need, like some people, letters of recommendation to you or from you? You yourselves are our letter, written on our hearts, known and read by everybody. You show that you are a letter from Christ, the result of our ministry, written not with ink but with the Spirit of the living God, not on tablets of stone but on tablets of human hearts" (2 Cor. 3:1-3).

"Known, yet regarded as unknown; dying, and yet we live on; beaten, and yet not killed; sorrowful, yet always rejoicing; poor, yet making many rich; having nothing, and yet possessing everything. We have spoken freely to you, Corinthians, and opened wide our hearts to you" (2 Cor. 6:9-11).

What is one word you would use to describe your life before faith in Jesus? __________

What word would you use to describe your life now as a follower of Christ? __________

NOTES

To the Leader:

Authenticity is a buzz word in many Christian circles. Everyone wants to be authentic. Yet many who have grown up in church are still uncertain as to what exactly it means to be authentic as a follower of Jesus.

See this lesson as a way to help learners grasp the true meaning of authenticity. For those investigating faith or new to Christianity, this is an exciting opportunity to envision a healthy view of faith. Seasoned believers will have a chance to rethink how they flesh out their faith in daily life.

Make sure the Scriptures referenced in Week 1 are the criteria by which learners define marks of authenticity.

Before the Session

1. Be prepared with definitions for the word *authentic.* Look the word up in a dictionary as well as in a thesaurus. Consider having access to a marker board or paper so you can visibly write out the definition of *authenticity* so people can see it during class discussion.
2. As a visual prop, bring any certificates of licensing you have with you to class. These could include a drivers or marriage license, certificate of qualification, and so forth.
3. Also consider bringing a scented candle and matches.

During the Session

1. State: *Define the word* ***authentic?*** Use your marker board or paper to jot down responses. Ask learners to think of words that are synonymous with the word *authenticity.* Use your visual prop as an optional illustration (see "Before the Session"). Explain that certificates and licenses verify authenticity. They point to the real thing. Refer to the introductory questions located in the "Introduction" section on page 6. Review each of the questions to focus learners on a specific discussion of authentic Christianity.
2. Remind learners that Week 1 reflects the genuine marks of an authentic Christian. Ask learners to list the five marks Stedman discussed throughout Week 1. Ask: *Did any one particular day catch your attention? Why?*
3. Together as a class read 2 Corinthians 2:14. Remind learners that three different marks are mentioned in this one verse. Ask learners to focus on the first mark mentioned—thankfulness. Ask: *What does it look like to live the "Thanks be to God" attitude that Paul reflected in his own life?* Explain that this thankfulness is typically hardest to grasp when we are struggling. Refer to the second activity in Day 1 on page 7: *How do you react to the idea that God will take our pain and bring about a "highly desirable end"? If possible, describe an example or an experience from your life to support your reaction.* Allow learners to share and discuss

NOTES

their thoughts and response to this exercise. Ask: *Where in your life right now do you need unquenchable optimism?*

4. Direct learners to review 2 Corinthians 2:14 again. Ask them to identify the second mark of authenticity—unvarying success. Ask: *What does is mean to say Jesus always leads in triumph?* Have a volunteer read Philippians 1:12-30. After reading this passage, allow learners time to consider how this passage relates to Paul's own ethic of unvarying success. Refer to the activities in Day 2 on page 10. After discussing these activities, ask: *What do you think you miss when you wallow in your own unfortunate circumstances?*
5. Ask: *What is the third mark of authenticity mentioned in 2 Corinthians 2:14-16?* Refer to the first activity in Day 3. Instruct learners to share their responses to this activity. Light the scented candle you brought to class. Ask learners to compare this candle with the concept of carrying the aroma of Christ. Ask: *What kind of aroma do you think people would say radiates from your life?*
6. Ask learners to review Day 4 and list aloud the four qualities of integrity found in 2 Corinthians 2:17. Ask: *Of these four qualities, which do you think is lacking most in our modern-day Christian experience?* Next, refer to the last activity in Day 4 on page 14. Encourage learners to share which of the four categories of integrity they need to work on the most. Brainstorm briefly as a class ways you can improve your level of integrity.
7. Assign two learners to read aloud 2 Corinthians 3:1-3 and 6:9-11. After these verses are read, ask learners to define what they think it means to speak of an undeniable reality. Ask: *How would you answer Paul's question about your own encounter with faith—"Are you any different since you came to Christ"?* (the first activity on p. 15). Then add: *If someone asked you to prove that God changed your life, what would you say?*
8. Conclude class by asking the activity questions in the margin of Day 5: *What is one word you would use to describe your life before faith in Jesus? What word would you use to describe your life now as a follower of Christ?* Encourage learners to share their responses to these activities. Challenge learners to identify one of the marks discussed in this lesson that they feel they need to work on. Allow time so people can pray for one another as they strive to embody the marks of authentic Christianity in their lives.

The Secret

The Source of Our Sufficiency

In your own words, how would you define the word *sufficiency*?

____

____

What things in life do you typically rely on yourself to attain?

____

What things in life do you rely on others for?

____

Which is generally easier for you—relying on self or depending on others? Why?

____

____

After listing the five marks of an authentic Christian, one might ask, "Who is a consistent model of these qualities?"

The question hangs in the air, waiting for an answer. Immediately a half dozen or so possibilities come to mind, for the question is so important that half the world's activity is devoted to finding an answer. Paul, however, does not leave us groping for an answer to this searching question. In 2 Corinthians 3:4–6 he gives us his forthright answer.

Paul puts the great secret before us in unmistakable terms: "This confidence is ours through Christ! Our sufficiency is from God!" Lest anyone miss the implications of that, he puts the same truth negatively: "Not that we are competent or sufficient in ourselves! No, our sufficiency comes from God alone." Nothing coming from us; everything coming from God! That is the secret of secrets—the secret of true fulfillment, satisfaction, and success.

To live with nothing coming from us and everything coming from God is to live in the Spirit. The Spirit continually gives Life with a capital *L*. This is the secret that produced the confident spirit that characterized Paul and empowered him to spread the fragrance of the knowledge of Christ everywhere he went.

If someone outside the Christian life asked you to describe the "Life" referenced in the above paragraph, what would you say?______________________

The apostle further indicates that the secret of an effective, meaningful life lies in what he calls "the new covenant." Jesus referred to this "new covenant" at the institution of the Lord's Supper (Luke 22:20), which is to remind us that Jesus died *for* us in order that He may live *in* us. His life in us is the power by which we live a true Christian life.

There are, according to Paul, two covenants at work in human life. One is the new covenant, which Paul would describe as "nothing coming from me, everything from God." This is in direct contrast to the old covenant, which could be described as "everything coming from me and nothing coming from God."

Which of the two covenants best describe you? _____

What needs to change in your life and mind-set in order to move you toward the "new covenant"?

____

How Paul Found the Secret

Since the apostle uses his own experience as the example of the kind of life he has in view, it will be helpful to trace the way and the time that he came to learn this transforming truth for himself. If you think it all came to him in that one dramatic moment in the dust of the Damascus road when he discovered the true identity of Jesus Christ and yielded himself to his lordly claims, then you are far from the truth. It is a great encouragement to many of us who struggle in the Christian life to learn that Paul also went through a period of probably ten years after his conversion before he began to live in the fullness of the new covenant. And it was during this time that, from God's point of view, he was an abject failure in living the Christian life!

Paul himself tells us in more detail what happened in his life. We find his description of that time in his Letter to the Galatians. Paul describes what happened to him after his conversion in Galatians 1:15–17.

"But when God, who set me apart from birth and called me by his grace, was pleased to reveal his Son in me so that I might preach him among the Gentiles, I did not consult any man, nor did I go up to Jerusalem to see those who were apostles before I was, but I went immediately into Arabia and later returned to Damascus" (Gal. 1:15-17).

What did he do in Arabia? Scripture doesn't tells us, but I don't think it is difficult to figure out. As a Pharisee and based on what he knew of the Scriptures, he had been convinced that Jesus of Nazareth was a fraud. Now he knew better—yet somehow, somewhere, he must work out the mental confusion this new discovery produced in him. Arabia supplied the opportunity. So into Arabia he went, the scrolls of the Old Testament tucked under his arm. As we might well surmise, he found Jesus on every page. How the old, familiar passages must have glowed with new light as, beginning with Moses and all the prophets, the Spirit of God interpreted to him the things that belonged to Jesus. It was no wonder that when he returned to Damascus he came "greatly strengthened." And no wonder, too, that Paul went into the same synagogues, armed with his newfound knowledge, and began proclaiming for the first time Jesus is the Son of God. In the Jewish houses of worship, he turned from passage to passage of the Jewish Scriptures and "proved" (Greek: "to knit together") that Jesus was the Christ, the Messiah foretold by the Old Testament.

Then things took a turn for the worse. To young Saul's chagrin the Jews of Damascus were not at all responsive to his powerful arguments. Luke tells us what happened in Acts 9:23–25.

Who has been unresponsive to your faith in Jesus and how does this typically make you feel?

____

What a burning humiliation to this dedicated young Christian! Paul had become—quite literally—a basket case! How humiliating to be let down over the wall in a basket like a common criminal escaping from the reach of the law! Once over the wall, he slips off into the darkness of the night, bewildered, humiliated, and thoroughly discouraged. He stated later that it was both the lowest point in his life and the beginning of the greatest discovery he ever made.

Where does he go from there? Luke tells us immediately in Acts 9:26. Paul's own account in Galatians 1:18–19 agrees with this exactly. How he managed to break through the fear barrier to see Peter and James is given us by Luke in Acts 9:27–29.

Once again the ardent young Christian is determined to persuade the Greek-speaking Jews that Jesus is the promised Messiah of the Old Testament. Once again a plot against his life is set in motion. Luke does not relate to us young Saul's reaction to the opposition he received when he preached to the Jerusalem Jews. But knowing his ambitious and dedicated heart, it must have been one of severe discouragement. At any rate, years later, Paul mentioned this event in his great defense to the Jerusalem mob when he was arrested in the temple precincts and saved from certain death only by the timely intervention of the Romans. In Acts 22 he tells us, "When I returned to Jerusalem and was praying at the temple, I fell into a trance and saw the Lord speaking. 'Quick!' he said to me. 'Leave Jerusalem immediately, because they will not accept your testimony about me' " (Acts 22:17–18).

How have past attempts to "persuade" others typically turned out?

____

How often was your attempt to persuade based on your own ability?

____

At this point Saul began to argue with Jesus: " 'Lord,' I replied, 'these men know that I went from one synagogue to another to imprison and beat those who believe in you. And when the blood of your martyr Stephen was shed, I stood there giving my approval and guarding the clothes of those who were killing him' " (Acts 22:19–20).

In these words Saul gave himself away. We can now see what he was depending on for success in his witnessing efforts. It is apparent that he saw himself as the one person who was eminently qualified to reach the Jews for Christ. His argument says in effect, "Lord, You don't understand this situation. If You send me out of Jerusalem, You are going to miss the opportunity of a lifetime. If anyone understands how these Jews think and reason, it is me. I was one of them. I speak their language. I know how they react. I understand their background. I too am an Israelite. Lord, don't send me away. I have what it takes to reach these men. Don't miss this opportunity!"

Paul was a strongly self-sufficient, qualified guy, and this definitely adversely affected his ability to connect with God. In the space below, indicate how your own sense of self-sufficiency, namely being "qualified," has affected your ability to experience God.

Jesus' answer is abrupt and to the point. Paul tells us himself, "Then the Lord said to me, 'Go; I will send you far away to the Gentiles' " (Acts 22:21). What a shattering blow! Luke tells us, "When the brothers learned of this [the plot to kill Saul], they took him down to Caesarea and sent him off to Tarsus" (Acts 9:30).

Tarsus was Paul's hometown. There is no tougher place to go as a Christian than back home. Paul had tried his best to serve his newfound Lord with all the ability and energy he could muster. But it amounted to exactly nothing. In fact, at this point, Luke records a rather astonishing thing after Paul's exile to Tarsus: "Then the church throughout Judea, Galilee and Samaria enjoyed a time of peace. It was strengthened; and encouraged by the Holy Spirit, it grew in numbers, living in the fear of the Lord" (Acts 9:31).

Why do you suppose Paul was having such a hard time?

____

Have you ever felt like a "dedicated disputer"?

____

The record shows that at first the Apostle Paul was not so much the dynamic history-changing missionary he later became. No, initially the Apostle Paul was really something of a "consecrated blunderer!" In his earnest, fervent, good-hearted way, he went about, preaching the gospel, and stirring up all kinds of anger and hostility among the Jews! When this "dedicated disputer" was eliminated—sent away to his hometown of Tarsus—the church finally had peace! It began to grow!

Saul goes off to Tarsus to nurse his wounds, his ego shattered and his plans dissolved in despair. For ten years he is not heard of again—not until an awakening breaks out in Antioch of Syria and the church in Jerusalem sends Barnabas down to investigate. When Barnabas finds "a great number of people [are being] brought to the Lord" (Acts 11:24), he knows help is needed and according to verses 25–26, "Barnabas went to Tarsus to look for Saul, and when he found him, he brought him to Antioch. So for a whole year Barnabas and Saul met with the church and taught great numbers of people." It was a different Saul who came to Antioch with Barnabas. Chastened, humbled, taught by the Spirit, he began to teach the Word of God, and from there launched into the great missionary thrust that would take him eventually to the limits of the Roman Empire and spread the gospel with explosive force throughout the world.

In the margin give an example from your life when you felt "chastened, humbled, and taught by the Spirit"?

____

How did this experience affect and change you?

____

Are You a Basket Case?

What made the difference? Writing to the Corinthians many years later Paul makes one brief reference to the event that triggered a line of teaching that would culminate in a clear understanding and acceptance of what he came to call "the new covenant." The Corinthian church had written to Paul and brazenly suggested to him that he would be more effective if he would boast once in awhile in his accomplishments. To this the apostle in 2 Corinthians 11:32–33 tells them what his boast is: "In Damascus the governor under King Aretas had the city of the Damascenes guarded in order to arrest me. But I was lowered in a basket from a window in the wall and slipped through his hands."

"That," says Paul, "is my boast. That is the greatest event of my life since my conversion. When I became a basket case, then I began to learn the truth that has changed my life and explains my power." What was that life-changing truth? Paul put it in his own words in Philippians 3:4–8. The word he uses for "consider them rubbish" refers to common, barnyard dung. What he once regarded as qualifying him to be a success before God and men (his ancestry, his orthodoxy, his morality, and his activity) he now regards as so much manure compared to depending on the working of Jesus Christ within him. He has learned how to shift from the old covenant (everything coming from me, nothing coming from God) to the new covenant (nothing coming from me, everything coming from God), which gives life. He is no longer highly qualified to be utterly useless but is able to say: "My sufficiency is from God, who has qualified me to be a minister of a new covenant."

"But whatever was to my profit I now consider loss for the sake of Christ" (Phil. 3:7).

How far or close do you think your life matches up to the last statement of the paragraph to the left?

____

What is your reason for feeling this way?

____

____

Have you become a basket case yet? Have you reached that place where you depend wholly on the Lord at work in you? That is where you learn the truth of the new covenant and nowhere else.

What would be your list of credentials, titles, accomplishments, and so forth? ____________________

How do these things affect your self-image? ________

____

How about your willingness to trust God? __________

____

Does it seem reasonable that you should treat your accomplishments as "backyard dung"? After all, you've probably worked hard from some of the credential and titles you hold. What do you think?

____

Two Faces of Glory

To help the Corinthians (and us) understand what he meant by "the old covenant" and "the new covenant" the Apostle Paul used two very helpful visual aids. They are borrowed from the story of the giving of the law from Mt. Sinai and the subsequent conduct of Moses with the people of Israel. He first calls attention to the glory of Moses' face in 2 Corinthians 3:7–8.

The old covenant, which Paul calls "a ministry that brought death," was aptly symbolized by the shining of Moses' face when he came down from the mountain with the law "engraved in letters on stone." There was a certain glory or splendor about the law. It attracted people and awakened their admiration and interest. That's what glory always does; it is captivating and attractive. To this day the law retains that attractiveness. All over the world the Ten Commandments are held in high regard, even by those who regularly break them (which includes us all). People pay lip service to them as the ideal of life, even though they may say they are impractical and impossible to keep.

But Paul emphasizes the even greater splendor of the new covenant. It is far more attractive and exciting than the law. Reliance on the old covenant cannot compare with life in the new. And just as the glory of the old covenant has its symbol (the shining face of Moses), so the new covenant has its symbol as well. Paul mentions it a little further on in the passage and obviously intended it to be set in contrast with the face of Moses. He says, "God, who said, 'Let light shine out of darkness,' made his light shine in our hearts to give us the light of the knowledge of the glory of God in the face of Christ" (2 Cor. 4:6).

Why do you think the glory of Moses, as described above, is so appealing to us? ______________________

What do you think of the statement "Reliance on the old covenant cannot compare with life in the new"?

____

Has this been your experience? ______________________

If someone asked you to describe how it feels to live according to the new covenant, what would you say?

____

Here, then, are the two splendors—the face of Moses and the face of Jesus Christ. Both are exciting; one much more than the other. They stand for the two covenants, or arrangements, by which human life is lived. Both have power to attract men, but one is a fading glory and the other is eternal. The unredeemed world lives continually by looking at the face of Moses. The Christian can live by either, but never both at the same time. It is always one or the other at any given moment of a Christian's life. In the true Christian's life, the activity of each moment derives its value from whether he is, at that moment, symbolically looking at the face of Moses or at the face of Jesus Christ.

In one sentence, how would you describe the glory of the old covenant?

How about the new covenant?

Which of these two covenants typically governs your spiritual experience?

____

What steps do you need to take to embrace the splendor found in the "face of Christ"?

____

____

The Trouble with Law

At this point we must seek to understand more clearly something of great importance. Someone may well raise the question, "Why does Paul link the old covenant with the law and call it a 'ministry that brought death'?"

In Romans 8:3 the apostle gives us the clue that explains this enigma: "What the law was powerless to do *in that it was weakened by the sinful nature,* God did by sending his own Son in the likeness of sinful man to be a sin offering" (emphasis added). The problem, therefore, is not the law; it is what the law must work with, that is, the flesh. The word *flesh* does not refer here to the meat and bones that make up the body, but is an equivalent term for fallen human nature—human nature acting apart from Christ. The law, in any of its forms, was needed and was given only because the flesh exists.

This helps us to see that the essential conflict between the old covenant (the face of Moses) and the new covenant (the face of Jesus Christ) is, in reality, the struggle between the flesh and the Spirit. Each of us is, in effect, a walking civil war. The flesh wars against the Spirit within us, just as Paul observed in Galatians 5:17. It is because of this inevitable tie between the flesh and the law that Paul, in 2 Corinthians, refers to the law as a "ministry that brought death" and says that "the letter kills."

How intense is the "civil war" within you . . . namely, the tension between the old and new covenants?

This, then, is the primary characteristic of the flesh—it is self-serving. It is God's life, misused. It can have all the outward appearance of the life of God—loving, working, forgiving, creating, serving—but with an inward motive that is aimed always and solely at the advancement of self. It thus becomes the rival of God—another god!

This is why fallen human beings, working in the energy of the flesh, can do many good deeds—good in the eyes of themselves and others around them. But God does not see them as good. He looks on the heart and not on the outward appearance, therefore He knows they are tainted right from the start.

If Jesus looked at your heart right now, what would He see? ______________________

There is a certain splendid attractiveness about the flesh, trying to be good. It strongly appeals to many, but it is like the shine on Moses' face—a fading splendor! But the splendor of the new covenant is far greater. It derives from the activity of Jesus Christ at work within humanity. It is perfectly acceptable to God. It is a delight to Him, for it is the activity of His beloved Son and will ever be characterized by His life—a life of genuine love, faithful work, and unreserved forgiveness; a life that is continually, freshly creative, and humbly given to service to others without thought of repayment or recognition.

Why are we so attracted to a religious person who seeks to "be good"? ______________________

If someone asked you to describe what Jesus offers—different from other religions—what would you say?

____

Of all the characteristics listed in the above paragraph, which seem strongest in your life?

____

Which seem to be lacking? ______________________

That is humanity as God intended humanity to be. That is the humble yet beautiful splendor of authentic Christianity.

How has the "flesh" revealed itself in your life?

____

How could observance of God's law be "self-serving"? ______________________

____

Why is there potential danger for us in solely seeking to follow the law as we live out our days?

____

Has faith in God ever felt like an advancement of self?

____

Based on your study of these lessons up to this point, write one sentence that describes what you are learning of the correlation between the new covenant and authentic Christianity.

NOTES

To the Leader:

The struggle for many Christians is a genuine desire to delve deep into faith in Jesus Christ. However, many are frustrated by failed attempts to make faith work in life. Some still come to church, because they know it is the right thing to do. Yet others grow weary and give up. Be sensitive to the fact that many of the learners in your class may be struggling with how to thrive in their faith. This lesson will help learners grasp the brilliant sufficiency that comes solely from Jesus.

Before the Session

Bring any form of an instruction manual into class (for an appliance, computer, piece of furniture that has to be assembled, etc.).

During the Session

1. Ask: *Have you ever been in a place, concerning your faith, where you felt like it simply didn't work? What made you feel this way?* Explain that we sometimes wish faith was like an instruction manual that simply told you what button to push or what piece to assemble to make faith work. (Show the instruction manuals.) Explain that faith doesn't work this way. We don't have such an instruction manual, but we do have something much better. We have God's Word, which introduces us to the secret of authentic faith. Allow someone to read aloud 2 Corinthians 3:4-6. Ask: *Based on this Scripture passage, how would you describe our source of sufficiency?* As a follow up question, ask: *What is the essential difference between the old and new covenants?* For additional discussion, direct learners to the last activity of Day 1 on page 19.
2. Ask: *As you read the description of Paul's life, described in Day 2, did you learn anything new about the life of Paul?* If time permits, review the passages cited in Day 2: Galatians 1:15-19; Acts 9:23-29; and Acts 22: 17-20. Explain that there is much we don't know about Paul's journey and growth. But it is clear that he had to go through a sort of spiritual "detox" from his old religious patterns. This didn't happen overnight. It took time, and Paul had to eventually learn the way of the "new covenant." Encourage learners to share their experiences of religious "detox." Explain that many of us have picked up bad habits within the church setting. Explain that we too must think hard about the tension that exists within us regarding the old and new covenants. Direct learners to look particularly at the activity in Day 2, page 22. Challenge learners to share their own experiences of being "chastened, humbled, and taught by the Spirit."
3. Read aloud Philippians 3:4-7. Ask: *What did Paul discover about himself and the secret to experiencing true faith? How does Paul's revelation relate*

NOTES

to the concept of the new covenant? Explain that Paul was definitely a man of credentials. Over the span of his life he had to learn that his credential meant nothing. Ask: *Is this a struggle for modern day Christians? Explain your response.* Ask learners to list aloud credentials that interfere with our ability to embrace Jesus as our sufficiency. Use the activity in Day 3 on the bottom of page 23 and the top of page 24 to facilitate discussion as to how we personally struggle with our own set of credentials.

4. Remind learners that Day 4 focused on 2 Corinthians 3:7-8. Ask: *How does this passage relate to the difference found between the old and new covenants?* Instruct learners to think about what the "glory of Moses" would look like in the context of our modern church culture. Refer to the activity in Day 4 on page 25 and ask learners to share their responses to those questions (or give them time to write responses to the questions in their books).
5. With reference to 2 Corinthians 3:7-8, review the contents of Day 5. Instruct learners to share what they learned about the law as they worked through this material. Ask: *Why did Paul see the law as a "ministry that brought death"? If this was the case, why are we still drawn to abide by the law to validate our spiritual life?* Refer to the activity in Day 5 on page 26 and ask learners to share their responses to the question: *How intense is the "civil war" within you . . . namely, the tension between the old and new covenants?* Assure learners that they are not alone if they've felt the struggle. Explain that it feels strange to realize that no set of rules can validate us before God. Yet we still try to validate ourselves before God—"Look at this God! I did this for You!" For a final application of this particular lesson refer to the second from the last paragraph of Day 5. Have someone read this paragraph (which begins with "There is a certain splendid attractiveness about the flesh"). Follow up by directing learners to review the activity immediately following this paragraph on page 27. Encourage learners to share what they wrote down.
6. As a final wrap up of Week 2, ask learners how they responded to the last marginal activity on page 27.

Death Versus Life

Life Versus Death

"Now if the ministry that brought death, which was engraved in letters on stone, came with glory, so that the Israelites could not look steadily at the face of Moses because of its glory, fading though it was, will not the ministry of the Spirit be even more glorious?" (2 Cor. 3:7-8).

Paul shows us a remarkable series of four contrasts in 2 Corinthians 3:7–11 so we can distinguish the result of trusting in the flesh from the result of trusting in the Spirit in our daily lives. When we learn to recognize which force is at work within us, then we will be ready to change from the flesh to the Spirit.

First, Paul contrasts the immediate effect produced by the flesh with that produced by the Spirit.

Read 2 Corinthians 3:7–8. What was Paul specifically referring to in 2 Corinthians 3:7?

____

What is being dispensed in the ministry of the Spirit? It is life! To depend on everything coming from you, in response to the demand of the law, produces immediate death. To depend on everything coming from God produces immediate life.

How would you define "life" as described by Pastor Stedman?

____

____

To think of death in terms of a funeral, as the end of existence, is to miss the point of what Paul is saying here. What is death? It is essentially a negative term meaning the absence of life. A doctor who examines an injured person does not look for signs of death; he checks for the signs of life. If he does not find them, he knows the person is dead. Life produces its own distinctive marks; death is the absence of those marks. That being so, the question we must really ask is: What is life?

Sometimes we hear a person say, "I'm really living!" What does that person mean? That he or she is experiencing great *enjoyment,* of course! Enjoyment is a part of life, as God intended it to be. Purpose, meaning, worth, fulfillment; all these are part of life. How about other qualities—

joy, peace, love, friendship, power? The moment we have these qualities, we are living Life with a capital *L*. Life full of love, joy, peace, long-suffering, gentleness, goodness, faith, meekness, self-control—that's living!

"But the fruit of the Spirit is love, joy, peace, patience, kindness, goodness, faithfulness, gentleness and self-control. Against such things there is no law" (Gal. 5:22-23).

In contrast then, what is death? It is the absence or opposite of those qualities of life. What is the absence of love? Hate, selfishness, and fear. What is the absence of joy? Misery, weariness of spirit, anger, hopelessness. Thus frustration, boredom, worry, hostility, jealousy, malice, loneliness, depression, self-pity—these are all marks of the absence of life. In short, they are forms of death. We do not need to wait till we die to experience these. For all too many of us, they are a major part of our experience while we yet live. They represent death in the midst of life.

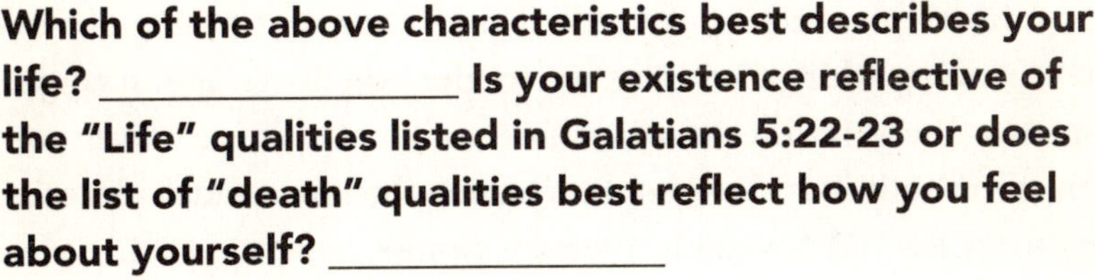

Which of the above characteristics best describes your life? ________________ Is your existence reflective of the "Life" qualities listed in Galatians 5:22-23 or does the list of "death" qualities best reflect how you feel about yourself? ________________

Where do these attitudes and passions come from, often when we least expect them? Jesus helps us answer these questions in Matthew 7:16–18. We think these negative qualities come from passing moods or changing circumstances. Both Jesus and Paul say no! They come from something deeper, something much more fundamental. They arise from a dependence on the old covenant, the "bad tree" that cannot produce good fruit. They reveal that we are unconsciously or consciously depending on "something coming from me" rather than "everything coming from God."

These negative feelings reveal the flesh in action. Not the flesh in the blatant display of evil we usually think of—drunkenness, rioting, adultery, thievery, murder, and the like—but the flesh in those subtler displays we often approve and even seek after—self-sufficiency, self-pity, self-centeredness.

How have the qualities of self-sufficiency, self-pity, and self-centeredness played a role in your own life?

____

Specifically, how do these things affect your quality of life? ________________________________

A tug-of-war exists within all of us who choose to follow Jesus. It is between the old and new covenants. Which is winning in your life right now? ______

What tips, based on the Scripture passages cited in this lesson, can you apply to get at living a life in light of the new covenant?

______

The presence of these marks of death gives us the clue as to when the old covenant is at work. Whenever these negative qualities are there, the old covenant is working, for that is what produces them. On the other hand, whenever the qualities of joy, trust, confidence, beauty, worth, and fulfillment are present, they can only come from the new covenant. It is the Spirit of God who produces them.

In these verses Paul reminds us there are two glories or splendors involved here. There is a certain glory about the "death" that the old covenant produces, but there is a greater glory about life. There is a certain attractiveness about the marks of death. We take a morbid pleasure in them. Have you ever caught yourself wallowing in a morass of self-pity and resisting all attempts to bring you out of it? You wanted to be left alone so you could have a good time feeling sorry for yourself. It gives a perverse feeling of pleasure.

The amazing thing is that we prefer these temporary, fleeting pleasures to the glory that accompanies real life. Often we naively assume we can enjoy both. But if we insist on having the momentary pleasure that comes from the old covenant, then we cannot have the lasting pleasure that comes from the new covenant. So the first contrast the apostle draws, by which we can recognize the old or new covenants in action, is that of the immediate effects produced in life.

Stones or Hearts?

The second contrast has to do with the material substance with which each is concerned. Twice in this passage Paul stresses the medium by which the old covenant came. The law was written on stones; the Spirit writes on human hearts. The old covenant is concerned with stones, with dead things; the new covenant is concerned with hearts, with living people.

One mark, therefore, of *false* Christianity is that it is always deeply concerned with the importance of *things:* stones, rituals, ceremonies, buildings, stained-glass windows, spires, organs, proper procedures. The emphasis is put on these at the expense of people. But the new covenant reverses this emphasis. People are the important matter. Things are useful only as they help or do not help people.

Look at Jesus. See how utterly careless He was about the precise regulations of the Pharisees when those regulations stood in the way of healing people. Even the Sabbath was set aside when it stood in the way of meeting the needs of people. Jesus said that His disciples ate grain on the Sabbath because the Sabbath was made for man, not man for the Sabbath. The ultimate concern of the new covenant is always for people. The old covenant puts things first.

Read Matthew 12:1-14. How does this story highlight the difference between the old and new covenant?

___

Look at verses 11-12. What do these verses teach us about the nature of God as He relates to us?

___

Is this the understanding or picture of God you've encountered in your experience as a Christian? ___

Why or why not? ___

The world of business and politics almost always operates on the basis of the old covenant. That is why money is usually more important than people. When vested interests are at stake, the rights of people usually suffer. Let a company face a drop in sales or production and what happens? Management takes up the axe and heads begin to roll, with little regard as to how those people will survive. Profits come first. And how much of this attitude is also seen in the church! Programs and customs are perpetuated, not because they meet needs, but because status and acceptance are at stake—a dead giveaway that dependence is on "everything coming from us" rather than "everything coming from God."

Profits or people—which comes first in your life? ___

What specifically needs to happen in your life so you shift yourself more toward a "people first" mentality?

___

Reflect on an experience you've had that reflects false Christianity.
Now reflect on an experience you've had that embodies authentic, new covenant Christianity.
What difference did you experience?

___

___

Guilt or Righteousness?

A third contrast, found in 2 Corinthians 3:9, marks the difference between freedom and guilt: "If the ministry that condemns men is glorious, how much more glorious is the ministry that brings righteousness!" Here we find another mark of the old covenant in action. It inevitably produces a sense of condemnation—or to use a more modern term, *guilt*. But the new covenant produces quite the reverse—the feeling engendered is one of righteousness.

Which word best describes your experience with Christianity—guilt or righteousness? ____________

What people and things influence in feeling one way or the other? ____________________________

Unfortunately, "righteousness" is one of those great biblical words that is often misunderstood today. Most of us think of it as "doing what is right," and certainly that is part of its meaning. But the essence of the term goes much deeper. Its basic meaning is "being what is right." One *does* what is right, because one *is* right—that is the biblical idea of righteousness. Righteousness is the quality of being acceptable to and accepted by God—fully and without reserve.

Perhaps we will get the true sense of it if we substitute the word *worth*. The righteous person is the one who has a sense of being valued. He is no longer troubled with guilt, inadequacy, or hostility. He does not strive to produce something to earn significance, for he feels accepted by God, pleasing to God. Therefore this person is free to reach out to others who hurt or are fearful or feel condemned because he is free of these feelings. To depend on "everything coming from God, nothing coming from me" produces that sense of worth. That is righteousness.

Do you find yourself motivated by a sense of being made righteous or is guilt a key motivator? __________

Which of these two factors are more of a key motivator in your life? ____________________________________

On the other hand, how many Christians live continually under a sense of condemnation? When the basis for our Christian activity is dependence on something coming from us (our personality, our will-power, our gifts, our money, our courage), there is no escape from a sense of guilt, for we can never be certain when we have done enough! Around the world that basis of performance is driving Christians into frenetic activity that can result in nothing but sheer exhaustion.

The frenzied activities of Christians have become a joke. Someone has revised the old nursery rhyme to read:

> Mary had a little lamb,
> 'Twas given her to keep;
> But then it joined the Baptist Church,
> And died for lack of sleep!

Many churches judge their success by the number of activities they offer. For many, it comes as a great shock to learn from Scripture that a church can be an utter failure before God and yet be occupied to the full every night of the week—teaching the right doctrines and doing the right things. On the other hand, a church whose people are living by the new covenant can also be fully occupied with many and varied activities. It is not the *level* of activity that marks the success or failure of a church. It is the source of that activity. Is it the flesh, or the Spirit?

React to the paragraph at the left. Do you agree or disagree? __________

Explain your response and cite any experiences you have had that validates your opinion in the space below.

Remember, there is a certain glory about the activity of the flesh that is very attractive to people. Dedicated activity always gives one a certain sense of worth—for a while! It produces a kind of self-approval that is very pleasant to experience—for awhile. Paul says that "the ministry that brought death, which was engraved in letters on stone, came with glory" (2 Cor. 3:7), yet it is far surpassed by the glory and splendor of the ministry of righteousness. In fact, the apostle enlarges on this. He says, "If the ministry that condemns men is glorious, how much more glorious is the ministry that brings righteousness! *For what was glorious has no glory now in comparison with the surpassing glory*" (vv. 9–10, emphasis added).

Galatians 2:20 reveals Paul's freedom in Christ. On a scale of 1 to 10 (1 being never and 10 being always), does this type of freedom show up in your life? ______

What would be different about your life right now if freedom in Christ played a more prominent role?

____

This is undoubtedly an oblique reference to Paul's own experience that we have already traced in a previous lesson. The pleasure he derived from his dependence on his ancestry, his orthodoxy, his morality, and his activity soon came to have "no glory now in comparison with the surpassing glory." To trust in Jesus Christ, at work in him, as he describes it in Galatians 2:20, is to experience a sense of fulfillment and worth that is infinitely beyond anything he had ever experienced before. It was to be free! Little did he care what men thought of him, since he was so fully aware of what God thought of him—in Christ. Little did he care what appraisal people (even other Christians) might make of his ministry, since he fully understood that whatever Christ did through him would be approved in the eyes of God.

Fading or Permanent?

The final contrast Paul draws relates closely to the previous one. He says, "If what was fading away came with glory, how much greater is the glory of that which lasts!" (2 Cor. 3:11). The contrast is clear. The old covenant produces that which fades away, but the new produces that which is permanent. When Moses came down from the mountain with his face aglow, he found that the glory faded. Relatively soon it disappeared completely, never to be recovered. But the glory of Jesus' face never changes. Those who are expecting Him to be at work through them in response to the demands that normal living makes upon them will experience *eternal* results. They will never fade or lose their value. They are treasure laid up in heaven—not on earth.

Once again Paul reminds us of the attractiveness that accompanies dependence on the flesh. Challenging people to rely on their natural resources and abilities can often whip up a tremendous wave of excitement and enthusiasm. From such a meeting everyone goes home saying, "Wow, what a tremendous meeting! I can't wait to get started on this new program. This year we are going to make it." But every experienced leader knows what will happen. Soon the enthusiasm will begin to ebb—it might not last beyond the next morning! Those who go around later to collect on some of the promises made will find that people have grown dull and apathetic. By next year it must all be done over again, with new approaches and more powerful presentations, in order to stir up the same degree of excitement and commitment. Sound familiar?

"But," you might say, "that's just human nature. It is only realism to take it into consideration and make plans to overcome such apathy." This statement is true—it is human nature. But it is *fallen* human nature: in other words, the flesh!

But have you ever met anyone who has learned to function on the basis of the new covenant? They don't need repeated meetings to whip up their enthusiasm. After 25 years they're still just as fresh and vital on the same job as they were the day they started.

Think about your own efforts to abide by the spirit of the old covenant. How have you felt the "fading" effect of this covenant?

____

Does the above description seem true of your own story as a Christian? __________ As you have lived out Christianity over the years, does your faith feel fresh and vital or is it fading? ______________ As you live your faith, what influences the way you feel?______________

____

The new covenant refreshes the spirit continually. When the human spirit weakens in the face of continued demand (as intended), it looks immediately to the indwelling God, to the fountain of living water, receiving vigor and vitality to meet the day's demands with eagerness and enthusiasm. People who live on that basis are a delight to work with. They do not require continual encouragement and outward motivation (though they fully appreciate the kind words people say to them), for they know the secret of their activity is "nothing coming from me but everything from God." That permanent glory never fades. The activity of the flesh is always a fading glory.

In two or three sentences, describe in the margin how your life looks and feels different as you abide by the freedom found in the new covenant. (If you feel like living by the new covenant is unfamiliar, describe what you think life ought to look like.)

After working through this exercise, pray and ask the Lord to help you make the new covenant a greater reality in your life.

The Big Push

With these four contrasts Paul seeks to impress us with the total inadequacy of the flesh, despite appearances, and the total adequacy of the Spirit, despite the evaluations of men, whether of ourselves or others. It is the energy of the flesh versus the power of the Spirit of life in Christ Jesus. If, as a Christian, you are seeking to live by your own resources rather than by the life of Jesus within you, you are like a man who goes down to buy a car and does not know that it comes equipped with a motor. Naturally, a man buying a car on that basis would have to push it home. When he gets there, he might invite his family out for a ride, so the wife gets in behind the wheel, the kids in the back seat, and he starts pushing from behind. At that point you might come along and ask, "How do you like your car?"

"Oh, it is a tremendous car. Look at the upholstery, and get an eyeful of this color, and, oh yes, listen to the horn—what a great horn this car has. But, I do find it rather exhausting! It goes downhill beautifully, but if there is even the slightest rise in the pavement, I find myself panting and struggling and groaning. It is very difficult to push it uphill."

"Well, my friend," you may say, "you do need help. You know, at our church we are having special meetings this week. Our speaker is speaking on the very subject you need to hear: 'How to Push a Car Successfully!' On Monday night he is going to show us how to push with the right shoulder. On Tuesday night he will illustrate the techniques of pushing with the left shoulder. On Wednesday night he has slides and an overhead projector to show us how to really get our back into the work and push. On Thursday night he has committees and workshops organized that will help us all push more effectively, and on Friday night there will be a great dedication service where we all come down in front to commit ourselves anew to the work of pushing cars. Come every night next week, and learn all there is to know about how to push a car successfully!"

That is exactly the way many Christians live today. We spend hours seeking to teach people how to mobilize all their human resources and try harder to get the job done for God. But all we are mobilizing is the flesh. We seek to build up their confidence in the power of numbers, the hidden resources of the human spirit, and the possibilities of a determined will.

But if we really wanted to help the man who is pushing his car, we would say something like this. "Look, come around here in front." We would lift up the hood and say to him, "Do you see this iron thing with all the wiggles coming out of it? Do you know what that is? It's a motor. A power plant. The maker of this car knew you would have the problem that you've been having and so he designed a power plant that would enable you to go uphill as easily as downhill. When you learn several simple things about operating the motor, you will begin to experience the power. Just turn this key and the motor will start. Then you pull down that lever and step on the pedal on the floor and away you go. You do the steering, but the motor supplies all the power. You don't have to push at all. Just sit back and you can go up the highest hills with as much ease and relaxation as if you were going downhill. You don't need to worry for the motor is equal to whatever demand you make."

Now that is what authentic Christianity is all about. God knew that we human beings aren't adequate in ourselves to meet the demands life makes on us so He supplied a power plant—the life of Jesus Himself. It is perfectly adequate for the task. Our part is to learn to operate it correctly, then make the choices necessary to steering. When we do, we experience the restfulness of activity in His strength. That is, indeed, a surpassing glory!

Which reflects your faith experience—pushing a car or discovering the motor? ______________________________

What does this car parable teach us about the difference between the old and new covenants?

____

What does this parable reveal about your own journey as a Christian?

____

Review 2 Corinthians 3:7-11. Ask God to teach you how to enjoy the blessing of His covenant.

NOTES

To the Leader:

Many Christians struggle internally with faith because they desire to see power visibly displayed as they live out their faith. Unfortunately, all they often have discovered is emptiness. Often they are insecure and unsure if God's power is in their lives. No doubt learners in your gathering have struggled or are struggling with the absence of power they feel regarding their faith. Pray that God will open up their hearts to discover the real, genuine power that exists in Jesus.

Before the Session

Bring in contrasting examples of two items—such as pictures of a small rowboat and a large shipping freighter or a small moped and a roaring Harley Davidson.

During the Session

1. Either show pictures of the props you brought to class or show the actual objects to the learners. Ask: *Which of the items I am showing you would you rather have? Why? Which one represents more power?* Explain that God, who is the most powerful force in the universe, gives our faith to us. Ask: *Why do we often see our faith as a weak and fading force? What contributes to this feeling (that is, that our faith feels like a moped instead of a roaring Harley)?*
2. Refer to 2 Corinthians 3:7-8. Ask: *What exactly is this passage telling us about faith?* Explain that Paul was contrasting the difference between death and life. Ask learners to define *death* and *life* according to what they read in Day 1. Have someone read aloud Galatians 5:22-23. Refer to the activity in Day 1 on the top of page 31. Ask learners to share their responses to those questions. Refer to the final activity in Day 1 and ask learners to share their responses. Emphasize that we are all in the same boat with this struggle. Encourage learners to state how they are dealing with the "tug-of-war" in their own life.
3. Read together as a class Matthew 12:1-14. After reading this passage aloud, ask learners to consider how this story from the life of Jesus relates to the tension that exists between the old and new covenants. Ask: *If you had to pick a character in the story of Matthew 12:1-14 who you easily identify with, who would it be? Why do you feel this way?* For additional follow-up discussion on this passage and the subject matter of Day 2, utilize the activities on the top of page 33 as a way to facilitate further discussion. Ask learners to agree or disagree with the following statement: "The world of business and politics almost always operates on the basis of the old covenant." Follow up with reflections

NOTES

from the final activity of Day 2 on the bottom of page 33. Encourage learners to share how they responded.

4. Ask: *Which word best describes your experience with Christianity—* guilt *or* righteousness? *What specific people and things motivate you to feel one way or the other?* (This is the first activity of Day 3 on p. 34.) Encourage learners to share how guilt has infected their own spiritual journey. Assure learners that guilt is a common part of many Christians' experiences with faith and that guilt creates great confusion regarding God's goodness and identity. Ask: *What does it mean to be made righteous?* Follow up by referring to the second activity in Day 3 on page 35. Encourage learners to be honest in sharing what their true motivation has been for faith in life. Ask a learner to read aloud Galatians 2:20. After the reading, ask: *How does this passage explain the process of making us righteous?* Follow up with: *Does this verse really make sense in your heart or is it merely head knowledge?*
5. Read 2 Corinthians 3:11 aloud. Ask: *How does this passage relate to the idea of fading faith versus an enduring faith?* Remind learners this verse describes Paul's understanding of the power found in Jesus versus the power found in following a bunch of religious laws. Direct learners to share how they responded to the activities of Day 4 on page 37. Remember that some of the learners, if not a majority, may feel the unsettled reality that their faith seems to be fading. Make sure that learners don't try to dodge this issue. Lead them into genuinely dealing with their sense of a fading faith. Use the above mentioned activity as a way to facilitate discussion on this matter. Ask: *How would you define a "permanent" faith? How does this look and feel?*
6. Ask: *So what are you pushing?* Refer to the car parable in Day 5. Ask learners to summarize the meaning and intent of this parable. Ask: *Which reflects your faith experience—pushing a car or discovering the motor? What does this car parable teach us about the difference between the old and new covenants? What does this parable reveal about your own journey as a Christian?* (These questions are found in Day 5 on p. 39.)
7. As a concluding action step, refer once again to the last activity of Day 5 on page 39—*Review 2 Corinthians 3:7-11. Ask God to teach you how to enjoy the blessing of His covenant.*

The Two Enemies

Veils Christians Wear

"Therefore, since we have such a hope, we are very bold" (2 Cor. 3:12).

How does 2 Corinthians 3:12 match up with your experience as a Christian?

Boldness! That is the inevitable result of trust in God, trust in the new covenant—everything coming from God, nothing coming from me. Paul has found the secret of *true* boldness by 2 Corinthians 3:12. This boldness is rooted in a sure hope, a conviction that God is ready to work in him. And since success does not depend any longer on his own dedication, zeal, wisdom, background or training, then he can be very bold. It is God who will do it, and He can be depended on not to fail.

Paul immediately goes on to say, "We are not like Moses, who would put a veil over his face to keep the Israelites from gazing at it while the radiance was fading away" (2 Cor. 3:13). Here we learn something about Moses the Old Testament does not reveal. Moses was not aware of the shining of his face when he came down from Mt. Sinai. Naturally it didn't take him long to learn. At first Moses put on the veil every morning because of the brightness of his face. But as time passed and the brightness faded to nothing more than a dim glow, he still wore the veil each day.

Now Paul raises the question: *Why?* Why did Moses keep the veil on his face after the glory had faded? His answer: Moses was *afraid.* Afraid of what? Afraid that the Israelites would see that the glory had faded! The mark of his privilege and status before God was disappearing, and Moses did not want anyone to know it. So he did what millions have done ever since, he hid the fact of his faded glory behind a facade, a veil. He did not let anyone see what was really going on inside.

Unfortunately, Christians are particularly susceptible to donning veils, especially those that seem to be forms of Christian virtue.

Why do Christians feel the need to wear a veil?

How about you? Are veils a reality for you? ________ Describe what the veils look like in your life.

____

Self-righteousness is a particularly noxious form of Christian pride. It seizes upon some biblical standard of conduct and takes pride in its own ability to measure up externally while conveniently overlooking any failure of the inner or thought life to conform. The end result is a smug, patronizing, and even nasty attitude toward anyone who does not meet the standard. Self-righteousness is also the sin of the person who nags another, for the nagger is focusing on a single point of conduct and ignores the areas in his or her own life where a similar failure is occurring.

Another common Christian veil is sensitivity or touchiness. People who are touchy or excessively sensitive are easily hurt by the words or actions of others. They must be handled with kid gloves lest they take offense. And when offended, they suffer agonies of spirit and tend to wallow in a morass of self-pity. Their explanation of such agony is always the "thoughtlessness" or "rudeness" of others, but in reality it is their own protest at not being given the attention or prominence that they're sure they deserve.

An impatient spirit can be a veil to hide the reality of what we are. It is often manifested to indicate importance or busyness. It frequently appears as a mark of zeal or dedication. But to be easily irritated, to frown readily, or reply sharply is a form of pride usually used to cover insecurity or a deep sense of inferiority. A self-justifying habit by people who can't stand to be misunderstood but who are forever explaining their actions reveals something similar.

But perhaps the most common veil employed by Christians is remoteness—the practice of keeping feelings and attitudes completely to oneself. Remoteness arises primarily from fear—the fear of being known for what one is. Often, though, it is described defensively as "reserve," "privacy," or "reticence." It is clearly a veil to keep others from seeing a fading glory and is a direct violation of such biblical commands as "confess your sins to each other and pray for each other so that you may be healed" (Jas. 5:16) and "Carry each other's burdens, and in this way you will fulfill the law of Christ" (Gal. 6:2).

Why is self-righteousness often a pervasive problem in our churches?

____

How have you been affected by this malady?

____

How have you seen the veil of sensitivity or touchiness in your own life or in the lives of others?

____

What were the effects of this "veil" on yourself and others?

____

What factors in our present day context contribute to a veil of impatience?

____

How has a veil of remoteness played a role in your experience as a Christian?

____

The flesh, or natural life, likes nothing better than to hide or disguise itself. We all tend to fear rejection if we are seen for what we are. The satanic lie is that in order to be liked or accepted we must appear capable or successful. Therefore we either project capability (the extrovert) or we seek to hide our failure (the introvert). The new covenant offers the opposite. If we will admit our inadequacy, we can have God's adequacy, and all we have sought vainly to produce (confidence, success, impact, integrity, and reality) is given to us at the point of our inability. The key is to take away the veil.

Which of the above mentioned "veils" do you need to work hardest on removing from your life? __________ Ask God to guide and empower you to remove the "veils" from your life!

"But whenever anyone turns to the Lord, the veil is taken away" (2 Cor. 3:16).

The Great Unveiling

When you read 2 Corinthians 3:14-18, what does it mean to be free from the veils?

____

How are veils removed?

____

Would you best describe your faith in terms of freedom? Why or why not? If not "freedom," what word would you use?

____

How can these veils be removed? The answer is clearly stated by Paul in 2 Corinthians 3:14–16. Only in Christ is the veil taken away! And as the apostle goes on to tell us, "Now the Lord is the Spirit, and where the Spirit of the Lord is, there is freedom" (v. 17). The apostle goes on to describe this freedom in glorious terms in verse 18. This continual beholding of the glory of the Lord is doing something to us. More and more areas of our conscious experience are coming under the full control of the Spirit, and we are therefore reflecting an increasing likeness to Jesus; we are being changed into His likeness from one degree of glory to another. This is what we often call "Christian growth" or "growing in grace." This is why it is possible for you habitually to walk in the Spirit in one area of life and yet have other areas of your life where the flesh is still unconquered and speech and attitudes are fleshly instead of Spirit-governed. But how encouraging to know that the Spirit will never give up the battle! He seeks in a thousand ways to invade each separate relationship of the soul, and gradually He is doing so.

New Covenant Ministry

In 2 Corinthians 4:2 Paul gives us a negative and positive description of a new covenant ministry. First, the negative: "We have renounced secret and shameful ways; we do not use deception, nor do we distort the word of God." In Paul's time there were persons who considered it necessary to produce instant and visible results so they could appear successful in ministry. It didn't matter whether the ministry was a public or private one, success rested on obtaining some visible sign of achievement. Consequently, they turned to what Paul calls "secret and shameful ways" to produce the desired results.

Similar activities of our own day suggest what these disgraceful tactics were. Undoubtedly they consisted of psychological gimmicks, pressure tactics, emotional pleas, and heavy-handed demands. They would also include high-powered promotional campaigns, self-advertising posters and handouts, and the continual emphasis on numbers as an indicator of success.

In straightforward fashion, Paul renounced all these psychological tricks to gain impressive results. Furthermore, he refused to practice deception or "cunning" as evidently many others were doing in his day. The thought behind *cunning* is a readiness to try anything. It conveys the idea of being unprincipled, without morals or scruples. It is simple expediency, justifying the means by the apparently good ends achieved.

A final state of dishonesty was reached by those who descended to actually tampering with the Word of God to obtain the appearance of success they desired. This was not an altering of the text of the Bible. It was, rather, a twisting of the meaning of Scripture or a misapplication of truth. None of these approaches is needed in a new covenant ministry, Paul declares. They mark the very antithesis of it, and the appearance of any of them in a ministry would indicate the indulgence of the flesh.

Give examples of how you've seen God's message manipulated, distorted, or misrepresented.

Why do you think we feel compelled to "sell" the gospel with gimmicks and other similar tactics?

____

In stark contrast to the multiplicity of evil is the simplicity of truth. In a great positive declaration, the apostle describes his own practice and the practice of all who labor in the liberty and sweetness of the new covenant: "by setting forth the truth plainly we commend ourselves to every man's conscience in the sight of God" (2 Cor. 4:2b). Nothing more is ever needed. The truth as it is in Jesus is so radical, so startling in its breadth of dimension, so universal, so relevant to human life everywhere that no psychological tricks are needed to prop it up and make it effective or interesting.

React to the last sentence of this paragraph. How does this statement relate to your own experience with faith?

____

The goal of Paul's proclamation is equally clear: "We commend ourselves to every man's conscience." To appeal to the conscience is to seek to capture the whole person—mentally, emotionally, and volitionally. It does not aim at mere intellectual agreement and certainly not at a shallow emotional commitment. Rather, it seeks to impress the conscience that commitment to Jesus is right; that is, in line with reality, and the only way to true fulfillment.

Finally, this is to be done "in the sight of God." This means with an awareness that God is watching all that is done, appraising it and seeking to correct it where needed. But the phrase suggests even more. Since the new covenant is "everything coming from God," it means the responsibility for results is placed squarely on God alone. This is what gives the spirit of the worker a sense of serenity and peace. He or she is free to be an instrument in God's hands.

Agree or disagree: "The responsibility for results is placed squarely on God alone." ____________

What does this mean? Do we have any part or influence regarding the results? Explain your response.

Why Don't All People Believe?

Ideally, if God is responsible for results and is desirous that all be saved, then whenever the gospel is preached or taught there should be many responses. But in actual practice, this is not always true. Why? To this implied question the apostle responds in 4:3–4.

"And even if our gospel is veiled, it is veiled to those who are perishing. The god of this age has blinded the minds of unbelievers, so that they cannot see the light of the gospel of the glory of Christ, who is the image of God" (2 Cor. 4:3-4).

What is your initial reaction to 2 Corinthians 4:3-4?

Once again the veil of pride appears in this discussion. The reference this time is not to the veils evangelicals employ but to those used by worldly men and women when they are confronted with the good news about Jesus, the veil that obscures their ability to perceive the truth. To them the gospel appears unrealistic, remote from real life, making its appeal only to those who have a streak of "religion" in them.

And here is where we glimpse the enemy without. As Paul puts it, "The god of this age [Satan] has blinded the minds of unbelievers." As always, Satan uses pride to blind their eyes. They are so confident of their own ability to handle life, so sure that they have what it takes to solve their problems. To them, therefore, Jesus appears to be dispensable, hardly worth considering. They fail to see that He stands at the center of life and that *all reality* derives its content from him. A superficial reading of the passage leaves the impression that their minds are blinded or veiled *after* they hear the gospel preached. But Paul declares that people are turned away from truth long *before* they hear the gospel because *they refuse to examine life realistically.*

Describe examples of veils you observe worldly men and women applying to the message of the gospel.

"For we do not preach ourselves, but Jesus Christ as Lord, and ourselves as your servants for Jesus' sake.
For God, who said, 'Let light shine out of darkness,' made his light shine in our hearts to give us the light of the knowledge of the glory of God in the face of Christ" (2 Cor. 4:5-6).

Read 2 Corinthians 4:5-6 and paraphrase it in the space below in one to two sentences.

Are these people whose minds are blinded without hope? Is there no way to reach them in their darkness? Paul's answer to that in 2 Corinthians 4:5–6 is magnificent.

Paul's argument is that the preaching of Jesus as Lord (the center and heart of all reality, the one in control of all events) is a message that is honored by God, and God is a being of incredible power and authority. In fact, He is the One who at creation commanded the light to *shine out* of darkness. Notice, He did not command the light to shine *into* the darkness—He literally commanded the darkness to produce light!

For this reason the Christian can always witness in hope, knowing that a sovereign God will work in resurrection power to call light out of darkness in many hearts. Notice that Paul is careful to keep his preaching sharply focused on the only subject God will honor by calling light out of darkness—that is, "We do not preach ourselves, but Jesus Christ as Lord, and ourselves as your servants for Jesus' sake" (v. 5). The danger in preaching is that all too often we offer ourselves as the remedy for people's needs. We speak about the church or Christian education or the Christian way of life, when all the time what people need is Jesus. Only Jesus is absolutely essential to life. When one encounters Him, all the other things will fall into their proper places. In view of this, the role of the Christian is that of a servant. The Christian is there to discover the needs of others and to do whatever his Master tells him to do to meet those needs. The Christian is, therefore, a servant "for Jesus' sake."

Who in your life is turned off to the gospel? Make a list of their names in the margin and claim the supernatural promise found in 2 Corinthians 4:1-6 as a promise of hope for those you listed.

Pots, Pressures, and Power

Notice two profoundly important facts in 2 Corinthians 4:7—the description of basic humanity and the revelation of the intent of God.

Paul first looks at the basic material of humanity with which God works, and he describes it as a lowly vessel. What are vessels for? They are essentially containers made to hold something. This verse of Scripture reminds us that we human beings were intended to contain something. What were we made to contain? The startling answer of the Bible is that we are made to contain God! The glory of our humanity is that it was intended to hold the Almighty. Lives without God are "empty lives," devoid of what they were meant to contain. The result is hollow men and women who display an outward shell of busyness and interest but inwardly they are nothing but an echoing emptiness.

"But we have this treasure in jars of clay to show that this all-surpassing power is from God and not from us" (2 Cor. 4:7).

Describe a time in your life when you felt like an empty vessel.

____

But the Christian is more than an empty vessel. The Christian has something within—or, more accurately, *Someone* within. We have a treasure in our clay pot! And more than a treasure—a *transcendent* power! That is humanity as God intended it to be. God intended that His great power, wisdom, and love should become visible in very ordinary and otherwise inconsequential people. This is the second great truth found in this verse of Scripture.

The only hope we have of realizing in this present life the glory God intended for us is to learn to draw upon the treasure within and be empowered by the power available.

Is it easy or hard for you to recognize in your life the "treasure" described in 2 Corinthians 4:7? __________ If hard, why do you think so? If easy, what specifically has helped you recognize the treasure?

____

How would you instruct someone to go about acquisitioning the "power available" that comes from God?

____

To show how immensely practical these biblical truths are, the apostle goes on to describe the way it works in the trenches of daily living in verses 8–9. All the pressures common to humanity are present in the life of a Christian. The purpose of the Christian life is not to escape dangers and difficulties but to demonstrate a different way of handling them. There must be trouble, or there can be no demonstration. Look at the four categories of trouble Paul describes:

1. *Afflictions:* "We are pressed on every side." These are the normal irritations of life that everyone faces—the bothersome, troublesome incidents that afflict us.

2. *Perplexities:* There will be many times of uncertainty in our lives, many occasions when we do not understand what to do, what to say, or why things happen the way they do.

3. *Persecutions:* The word *persecution* covers the entire range of deliberate offenses against Christians from slight ostracisms, cold shoulders, and critical remarks to smears on reputations, hindrances to ministry, personal and bodily attacks, and even torture and death.

4. *Catastrophes:* "Struck down!" This phrase refers to the stunning, shattering blows that seem to come to us out of the blue—cancer, fatal accidents, a heart attack, riot, war, earthquakes, Alzheimer's disease, insanity. Christians are not protected from these catastrophic events. They are terrible experiences that severely try our faith and leave us frightened and baffled.

Which of these four categories listed above has had (or is having) an effect on your life?__________________

But look at the reactions to these trials Paul describes. "We are hard pressed on every side, *but not crushed.* Perplexed, *but not in despair.* Persecuted, *but not abandoned.* Struck down, *but not destroyed*" (emphasis added). For Christians there is a power within, a transcendent power, different from anything else, that keeps pushing back with greater pressure against whatever comes from without, so that we are not crushed, despairing, forsaken, or destroyed.

When you honestly evaluate your own trials, do you come to the same conclusion as Paul did about his trials? Why or why not? Respond in the margin.

This power within was given to us for the very purpose of handling life's afflictions. We are exposed to them so that we might demonstrate a different reaction than one that would come from a person of the world. Our neighbors, watching us, will find us difficult to explain, and it is only when we baffle them that we are likely to impress them with the advantage our faith gives. There will be a quality about us that can be explained only in terms of God at work. It must be evident that the power belongs to God and not to us.

When we ask ourselves whether this actually *is* the reaction of Christians to the normal trials of life, we must hang our heads in shame. All too often we react exactly as the unbelievers around us—and sometimes not as well.

So in verses 10–11 the apostle brings us the key to the life of Jesus being manifest in our mortal bodies right now in time. Two factors can produce it. One is an inner attitude to which we must consent (v. 10). The other is an outward circumstance into which we are placed (v. 11). First, the key to experiencing the life of Jesus is our willingness to accept the implications of His death—that we "always carry around in our body the death of Jesus." If I welcome the cross and see that it has already put to death the flesh rising within me so that it can have no power over me, then I find myself able to say no to its cry for expression. I can then turn instead to the Lord Jesus with the full expectation that as I will to do what He tells me to do in these circumstances, He will be at work in me to enable me to do it. Thus the life of Jesus will be manifest in my mortal life.

The second factor in verse 11 that produces the life of Jesus in us is something done to us. We have no choice in this second matter. We are being given up to death. This refers to those circumstances of trial and pressure into which God puts us to force us to abandon trust in the flesh and lean wholly on the Spirit of Christ.

This is why pressures and problems arise in our lives. The God who loves us is delivering us up to death in order that we might trust, not in happy circumstances or in pleasant surroundings, but in the Lord of life who lives within. Through our circumstances we are forced to *experience* this so that the treasure within might enrich us and the power within demonstrate before a watching world a totally new and different way of life. All this has an effect far beyond one individual life; it redounds to the glory of God, as the apostle points out in verses 12–15.

Complete the activities in the margin to the right.

Based on 2 Corinthians 4:7-15, why is our faith typically more effective as we walk through trials?

____

____

Regarding your own personal trials, how does your outlook need to change to grasp the blessings and power Paul described in 2 Corinthians 4?

____

____

NOTES

To the Leader:

We all conjure up images of what we want people to think about us. We wear masks or veils that hide certain things and also give off a false impression about who we really are. All this is often the result of our own insecurities. We are nervous about who we really are and would rather give people what we think they want out of us. As a teacher, be sensitive to the fact that learners in your group all face this struggle of insecurity within themselves. Help learners discover the power of enjoying God's way, which requires no veils!

Before the Session

1. Obtain any mask that hides features on your face.
2. Bring a ceramic jar.

During the Session

1. As you begin class, approach learners with the mask on your face. Begin welcoming people and give a review of what you've been doing in this study of authentic Christianity. After a while, ask: *Is anyone having a hard time with me wearing this mask? Why does it bother you?* After learners have had time to discuss their reaction to the mask, explain that we often wear masks in the ways we present ourselves to others. We are typically hiding something. Instruct learners to read 2 Corinthians 3:12-13. Ask: *How did Moses' veil resemble a mask? Why do you suppose Moses felt compelled to wear a mask?* Refer to the activity in Day 1 on pages 42-43. Ask learners to share how they responded. Continue by asking learners to list the different forms of "veils" described in Day 1. Ask: *Which of these veils do you feel like you struggle with?*
2. Read 2 Corinthians 3:14-18. Ask: *Does the reality described in this Bible passage ring true in your life?* Follow up by asking: *What is the key to being unveiled? Has this worked for you in the past? Why or why not?* After briefly reviewing learners' responses and referencing any of the other material in Day 2, it would be most appropriate to pause and pray for one another. Lead learners in a time of prayer, asking God to do what He promised in 2 Corinthians 3:16.
3. Explain that in Day 3 the lesson is focused on the amazing way God works through the new covenant. Yet we still try to control God's message in the world. Ask: *How does 2 Corinthians 4:1-2 describe age-old methods employed by people to control God's message? Why do you suppose we try to control God's message and power?* Refer to the first and second activities in Day 3 on pages 45-46. Follow the flow of Day 3's content. Move learners to think about the right way to go about faith and ministry—"in the sight of God." Ask: *Is it easy to leave the responsi-*

NOTES

bility of results squarely on God? Why or why not? How much of a role do you think we have in God's plan to reach people?

4. Transition into discussion of Day 4's topic by having someone read aloud 2 Corinthians 4:3-4. Ask: *How does this passage relate to the big picture of God's plan to reach people with His message of hope?* Ask learners to think about their reactions to 2 Corinthians 4:3-4 based on their responses to the first activity of Day 4 on page 47. After learners share their thoughts, direct discussion once again toward the veils worldly people apply to themselves. Ask learners to consider how these veils affect their ability to embrace faith. Have someone read aloud 2 Corinthians 4:5-6. Ask: *What hope does this passage offer us concerning our sharing the message of the gospel with people in the world?* Conclude this section of discussion by allowing learners to share how they responded to the last activity of Day 4 on page 48. If appropriate, this may be another opportunity to pray as a group for the people mentioned on the learners' lists.
5. Show everyone the ceramic jar (see "Before the Session"). After showing everyone the jar, have someone read aloud 2 Corinthians 4:7-12. Then ask: *What is the meaning of the jar?* Refer to the first activity in Day 5 on page 49. Allow learners to help paint a picture of what it feels like to be the "empty vessel" Paul described. Ask learners to consider how God has empowered them to do amazing things. Encourage learners to share their experiences. Ask: *Are you OK being an empty vessel? What in life tells you to think otherwise?* To summarize, refer to the second activity of Day 5 on page 49. Allow learners to describe what it feels like to have the "treasure" of God visibly active in their lives.
6. Trouble will come. Learners must recognize that faith in Jesus is not an inoculation against hard times. Ask: *How does the "treasure" of Christ help you weather the hard times?* Refer to the four categories of trouble listed in Day 5. Allow learners to share how they responded to the third and fourth activities of Day 5 on page 50. Ask learners to share how troubles have affected their faith journey. Provide time for people to share and talk this issue out. Be ready for people who haven't quite sorted through their confusion about hard times. Direct the conversation back to 2 Corinthians 4:7-15. Conclude by allowing learners to share how they responded to the last activity of Day 5 in the margin on page 51. Pray as a group regarding the different subjects raised in this discussion.

Time and Eternity

Something Greater Is Coming

We have already seen that authentic Christianity is far more than a "pie in the sky, by and by" religion. It is magnificently designed for life on earth, right now, with all its pressures and problems, its joys and tears. But there is yet more for us to experience. God has prepared something incomprehensibly beautiful for those who love Him and trust Him—something that lies beyond time, something so beautiful and vast and breathtaking that only eternity is big enough to contain it. The Apostle Paul tells us about the wonders of eternity in 2 Corinthians 4:16–18.

Based on your reading of 2 Corinthians 4:16-18, how would you describe eternity?

____

____

Paul states plainly that what we are going through now is only preparing us for something yet to come—something so glorious and so different from what we have known that it is beyond all comparison. This is the Christian hope. It is more than merely looking on to life beyond the grave. It declares that everything that happens to us in this life is directly related to what is coming—in fact, is getting us ready for it. Nothing, then, is purposeless or futile in our present experience. It is all necessary to the ultimate end.

On a scale of 1 to 10 (1 being never and 10 being always), how often do you find yourself focusing on eternity? ______________

The apostle suggests three aspects of the Christian life indicate that something much greater is coming. First, there is the daily inner renewal. "Though outwardly we are wasting away," Paul says in 2 Corinthians 4:16, "yet inwardly we are being renewed day by day." The sharp contrast he draws is between the effects of aging upon the body—particularly our lessening physical power and approaching death—and the increase of wisdom and the mellowing of love that mark the spirit of one who walks with God.

What is happening? The outer man is losing the battle; the strength of youth falters and fades, the night is coming on. But the inner man is reaching out to light, growing in strength and beauty. This inner renewal is another way of describing the new covenant in action. The law of sin and death is destroying the body; the law of the Spirit of life in Christ Jesus is renewing the spirit and also the soul "with ever-increasing glory." To see this happening in oneself or in another is to be convinced that something wonderful lies ahead.

How do you see 2 Corinthians 4:16 happening in your own life?

____

Identify areas of life where you feel like you are "wasting away" and, in contrast, identify areas where you feel like you are "being renewed."

Wasting Away **Being Renewed**

How do you typically react to your trials?

____

Is Paul's optimism about trials easy or hard to stomach? Why do you feel this way?

____

____

Furthermore in verse 17, the apostle stoutly declares that our trials and hardships actually produce the glory to come! He was aware of something we often forget. He knew that these painful trials were actually preparing the "eternal glory that far outweighs them all." Notice he does not say that these trials were preparing him for the glory. While that was true, it wasn't what he said here. The trials were creating the glory!

It seems clear, then, that something tremendous is ahead. Not only does daily inner renewal suggest it, and our present affliction is preparing it, but the very nature of faith itself guarantees it. "So we fix our eyes not on what is seen, but on what is unseen. For what is seen is temporary, but what is unseen is eternal" (2 Cor. 4:18). Paul's argument here is very simple. The visible things of this life are but transient manifestations of abiding realities that cannot now be seen. If the transient form can exist, surely the reality behind it exists. The truly important thing is not the passing form but the eternal reality.

Based on 2 Corinthians 4:16-18, brainstorm how you can make the unseen eternal reality a stronger part of your daily routine. Write your ideas in the margin.

The Best Is Yet to Be

In 2 Corinthians 5:1–4 Paul describes the weight of glory in more explicit terms.

"A building from God"? "Not built by human hands"? "Our heavenly dwelling"? What do these expressions refer to? They are obviously set in direct contrast to the earthly tent we live in, our present body of flesh and bones. But before we take a closer look at these phrases, note how definite and certain Paul is. See how he begins: "We know. . . ." There is nothing uncertain about it at all.

Do you approach discussions about eternity with the same confidence Paul held? Why or why not?

What do we know? First, says Paul, we know that we now live in an earthly tent. Twice he calls the present body a tent. Tents are usually temporary dwellings.

Further, he says that in this tent we both groan and sigh. Do you ever listen to yourself when you get up in the morning? Do you ever groan? The tent is beginning to sag. The cords are loosening and the pegs are growing wobbly. Sometimes we long for something more than this body offers.

In contrast to this temporary tent in which we now live, the apostle describes the permanent dwelling waiting for us when we die. It is "a building from God, an eternal house in heaven, not built by human hands." This is the indescribable "ever-increasing glory" now being prepared for us by the trials and hardships we experience. If the present tent is our earthly body, then surely this permanent dwelling is the resurrection body Paul described in 1 Corinthians 15:42–44.

If the apostle can describe our physical body as a *tent*, then it is surely fitting to describe the resurrection body as a *house*. A tent is temporary; a house is permanent. When we die, we will move from the temporary to the permanent; from the tent to the house, eternal in the heavens.

Twice in 2 Corinthians 5:5–8 Paul says that a clear view of the coming glory should mean that our present life is marked with good courage. He gives two reasons for this. First, in preparing us for the glory to come God has given us the Holy Spirit as His guarantee. We do not need to doubt that the resurrection of our body is ahead, for the presence within us of the Spirit of resurrection makes it sure.

The second reason for confidence in the present hour is that though the resurrection life will be amazing beyond description, it is nevertheless true that we are learning how to handle the resurrection body by the way we handle our present body now.

What is it we are learning now that will be so necessary then? It is to walk by faith and not by sight! That is the operative principle of eternity, and we must learn it here.

It is for this reason that Paul uses the term "at home" to describe both our present experience in an earthly body and the coming experience when we are "with the Lord." We are now "at home" in the body, though away from the Lord. Then we shall be away from the body, but "at home" with the Lord. In either case, we are "at home."

All our tenderest associations gather around the word *home*. It is where we feel relaxed, at ease, natural. And when we step into the stunning glory awaiting us, we will feel the same way—at home, relaxed, at ease. At home, here in the body, we are learning to walk by faith in a way that feels natural and comfortable. At home with the Lord, it will be the same.

"So will it be with the resurrection of the dead. The body that is sown is perishable,
it is raised imperishable;
it is sown in dishonor,
it is raised in glory;
it is sown in weakness,
it is raised in power;
it is sown a natural body, it is raised a spiritual body. If there is a natural body, there is also a spiritual body" (1 Cor. 15:42-44).

What assumptions can we make about our eternal existence based on 2 Corinthians 5:1-4 and 1 Corinthians 15:42-44?

____

If you focused on your eternal destiny more than you presently do, what do you think would look different about your life? ______________________________

What risks would you take? ___________________

Where in life would you feel more confident? ______

How would your priorities change? _____________

How would your life goals change? _____________

The First Motivating Factor

When you wake in the morning, how often is your routine initially shaped by a desire to please God?

____

What generally motivates you in life?

____

"So we make it our goal to please him," writes Paul in 2 Corinthians 5:9, "whether we are at home in the body or away from it." Pleasing God is the proper occupation of the Christian for both time and eternity.

The real problem of the Christian life is not how to discover the will of God or what will please Him. When the soul swings in the balance between truth and error, good and evil, what will tip the scale in the right direction? That is the real problem. It is the issue of *motivation.*

As with everything else in the Christian life, God has not left us without help at this point. Two powerful forces act upon us to stabilize our wavering wills and draw us back from the alluring brink. To choose is our inherent human function, but to choose *rightly* demands that a force operate within us that will firmly turn us and propel us in the right direction. Paul describes these forces to us. The first, perhaps rather surprisingly, is *fear,* as Paul indicates in 2 Corinthians 5:10–11.

Based on 2 Corinthians 5:10-11, how would you define the word *fear*? How does fear affect the way you prioritize your day?

____

Somehow the idea has grown among Christians that fear is an improper motive; that, if it is accepted at all, it is base and inferior. But Scripture never takes that position. Everywhere, from Genesis to Revelation, and especially in Genesis and Revelation, the fear of the Lord is extolled as a very proper and highly desirable motive for living. In fact, it is regarded as foundational: "The fear of the LORD is the beginning of knowledge, but fools despise wisdom and discipline" (Prov. 1:7). The psalmist exhorts us, "Fear the LORD, you his saints, for those who fear him lack nothing" (Ps. 34:9), and declares that a man reaches a stage of great danger when there is "no fear of God before his eyes" (36:1). It should not surprise us, therefore, that Paul speaks first of fear when he sets before us the great motives of life.

But what comes to mind when we think of fearing God? Is it some abject, cringing, expression of terror? No, such fear is inspired by guilt, and guilt has absolutely no place in a believer's relationship to God. The fear of which Paul speaks is something that is still there when a believer stands as a son before his loving Father, with a bold and confident spirit, making his requests known to him. It is a fear that finds its focus at the judgment seat of Christ.

Read 1 Corinthians 3:11-15 and 2 Corinthians 5:10. Describe God's judgment based on this passage.

____

____

This judgment tribunal is presented in Scripture as awaiting the believer who steps out of time into eternity. It is a time when "each one may receive what is due him for the things done while in the body, whether good or bad" (2 Cor. 5:10). This seems to suggest an occasion when our entire earthly life passes in review before us and we learn—perhaps for the first time!—what has been pleasing to God and what has not. It will undoubtedly be a time of great surprises. Many things we felt were acceptable to God and profitable to us will be found to be spoiled by improper or wrongful dependence. At the same time, God will single out many forgotten or seemingly insignificant acts as greatly pleasing to Him. Paul also speaks of this in 1 Corinthians 3:11–15.

How does the idea of God's judgment feel to you?

____

The "fear of the Lord" that Paul connects with this sobering judgment comes from an awareness that God cannot be fooled or deceived in any way. It springs from the fact that God views us with stark and naked realism, and that since He is no respecter of persons, we cannot count on privilege or favor for some special consideration before Him. He is not swayed by our emotional pleas nor moved by our tears to change His evaluation. Our explanations and justifications made so easily before ourselves

What shapes your perception of God's judgment?

____

or other people will die unuttered on our lips in the presence of Christ's immutable majesty. His judgment will be inescapable and without appeal.

It is this truth—the certainty that he will one day face the searching gaze of his Lord and Savior—that motivates Paul to serve Jesus and persuade men.

I believe that fear is deep within each of us. It has been put there by our Creator. No one wants to waste his or her life. When we understand the terms by which the value of that life is measured, we find it to be a great force to help us choose the right and reject the wrong. "What we are is plain to God, and I hope it is also plain to your conscience" (2 Cor. 5:11). Thus Paul seeks to persuade the Corinthians to walk as he walked with the bright light of the judgment seat of Christ on his path.

How can the fear of God and His judgment serve to motivate you in a healthy way as a follower of Jesus Christ?____________________________________

Does anything about this session on fear unsettle or disturb you? ____________________________________

Read 2 Corinthians 5:10-11 and 1 Corinthians 3:11-15 again. Ask God to show you a proper perspective regarding what it means to fear Him.

The Supreme Motive

Read 2 Corinthians 5:12-15. According to Paul, what is the chief motivator?

____

But there is a motive even greater than the motive of fear. Another force at work in our lives has power to move us even when the fear of wasting our lives leaves us unmoved (as it sometimes will). Paul now goes on to declare that greatest of all motives in 2 Corinthians 5:12–15.

Paul's behavior as a Christian was a source of bafflement to many at the church in Corinth. They could not understand his approach, and his motives were forever being questioned. His actions seemed strange to them because they didn't understand the new covenant. They expected him to act and react to situations just as they did—and they were confused and baffled when he did not conform. It is clear from this passage and others in the Corinthian letters that they expected him to boast of his exploits on behalf of Christ and to find subtle ways to commend himself before them, for this is what they did. But now he insists he is not doing this.

Rather, he explains that the force prompting him to act contrary to the usual ways of the world is not arising from a secret ambition for position. It originates from Christ within: "Christ's love compels us," urges us, drives us (v. 14).

Even though many people found it hard to explain Paul's actions, Paul could state clearly that his own objective was right. All of his behavior, whether crazy or sane, was focused on serving Christ and influencing people for Christ. Paul's goal could be anticipated when it was understood that the *love of Christ* urged him on. His actions were the actions of love, directed to the glory of God and the service of people, never for the advancement of self!

Think about the influence of God's love in your life right now. How does that love affect the way you live with regard to different people?

How about with regard to your job or to your church?

Now, *that* is always highly suspicious behavior! The person who has no axe to grind, no angle for his own profit, is behaving very strangely. The world expects people to "look out for Number One." The world also knows that everyone who is smart hides his self-interest until the last possible moment. He always *appears* to be concerned for the welfare of others, even while he is trying to manipulate the situation to his own advantage. That is why one frequently hears, "OK, what's your angle?" or "All right, what's the catch?" Most Christians also reflect this view, despite their high-sounding "Christianese."

Finding someone who consistently, in varying circumstances, behaves contrary to this basic human principle may cause some to be perplexed and unbelieving. What is the answer? "Love is the explanation," Paul says in effect. "The love of Christ presses us, urges us on, takes hold of us and overpowers our natural self-interest, and makes us act contrary to nature."

Why do you think, based on Paul's teaching, love is the greatest of all motivations?

How influential is the love of Christ in motivating your own spiritual life? If helpful, use the scale below to identify how much of a force the love of God is in your faith.

|____|____|____|____|____|____|____|____|____|

Heavily influential **Nonissue**

But There Is More

A death and a resurrection have occurred, Paul argues. "We are convinced that one died for all, and therefore all died." When Christ became what we are, He died, and, therefore, we who are in Christ have died with Him. The natural life has been shown to be worthless, totally unprofitable.

But there is more. "And he died for all, that those who live should *no longer live for themselves* but for him who died for them and was raised again" (v. 15, emphasis added). If we died with Him, we also rose with Him, and the risen life we now live is different from the old life. It is no longer self-centered, loving itself supremely. It is outward-directed. It reaches out to others naturally and without self-consciousness. It is not a put-on but real. Whenever we yield to the love of Christ, says Paul, that is the way we act, and His love is the reason we act that way. Once we have yielded to that love we cannot help being self-giving, for that is the way His love is. The love of Christ controls us.

Love makes obedience easy; it is the delight of love to do what the loved one desires. Therefore, when the heart grows dull and obedience is difficult, the proper response of the Christian is not to grit his teeth and decide to tough it out but to remember who it is that asks this of him and then for His sake to do it. When a Christian responds this way, he will find to his amazement that his own attitude has changed. A new outlook is born within him. That is what Paul describes in verses 16–17.

"So from now on we regard no one from a worldly point of view. Though we once regarded Christ in this way, we do so no longer. Therefore, if anyone is in Christ, he is a new creation; the old has gone, the new has come!" (2 Cor. 5:16-17).

Based on 2 Corinthians 5:17-18, how would you describe yourself in terms of a "new creation"?

____

Perhaps the clearest evidence that the new covenant is in operation is the change it makes in our view of others. No longer does position, caste, color, sex, or wealth matter. Everyone is seen to be of infinite worth because he or she is made in the image of God and can be redeemed through Christ. Nothing else really matters.

Yes, life as a Christian is totally, radically, different. Impelled by the twin motives of *the fear of God* and *the love of Christ,* it goes counter to the normal impulses of life. Right in the midst of the decay of the old creation, the new is rising. Eternity is invading time. Urged on, driven, and mastered by love, we will continue to swim against the current of this darkening age until the day breaks and the shadows flee.

Why is there a need for both "fear of God" and the "love of Christ"?

____

How will a balance of "fear" and "love" help you in the easy times?

____

How about the hard times? ______________________

Which of these two motivators do you need more of in this season of your life?

____

That is authentic Christianity. You find it under the worst, most horrifying circumstances imaginable. We should certainly be able to find it in our homes and our churches today.

NOTES

To the Leader:

A crisis of belief for many Christians comes when they wrestle with why they do what they do. What is their motivation? For some, faith was something they were told to do. For others, it was merely inherited or passed down from other family members. When cornered, some Christians couldn't really tell you why they follow Jesus. This lesson is a terrific way to spark discussion about the true motives for living out faith.

Before the Session

Bring some form of exercise equipment to class—such as a hand weight, exercise ball, and so forth.

During the Session

1. Pull out the piece of exercise equipment you brought to class (see "Before the Session"). Explain that most of us don't like the idea of getting up early in the morning or going after work to exercise. Yet many of us do exercise. Ask learners to share reasons why they choose to exercise. Motivations could include athletic training, health concerns, losing weight, enhancing one's appearance, and so forth. Explain there are a lot of things that motivate us in life. Ask: *What are the motivating forces and influences in your life?* Next, direct discussion toward the specific reasons we choose to have faith in Jesus. Ask learners to brainstorm a list of reasons they think people choose faith.
2. Ask someone to read aloud 2 Corinthians 4:16-18. Ask: *How does this verse relate to our motivation for following Jesus?* After learners have identified eternity as a key issue in this passage, ask: *Is it easy to fathom a future in eternity? Why or why not?* Refer to the activity of Day 1 on page 54. Encourage learners to share their responses.
3. Have fun with your discussion regarding 2 Corinthians 4:16. In a light tone, allow learners to describe how the aging process affects them. Don't let this discussion get glum. Instead, focus on the fact that we simply age and parts of our bodies don't work like they used to. Next, shift into a discussion of what it means to say that we are renewed on the inside. Ask: *How would you describe the inward process of renewal in your life?* Refer to the activity in Day 1 on page 55 for further dialogue about how the truth of this passage plays out in someone's life.
4. Focus attention on 2 Corinthians 4:17-18. Ask learners to share how this passage can serve as an encouragement in their lives. Refer to the final activity in Day 1 on page 56. Say: *With regard to 2 Corinthians 4:16-18, brainstorm ideas how you can make the unseen eternal reality a stronger part of your daily routine.*

NOTES

5. Direct learners to turn their attention to Day 2's content. Read aloud 2 Corinthians 5:1-5 and 1 Corinthians 15:42-44. Refer to the first activity in Day 2 on page 56. Ask learners to share how they responded to the question. Explain that an eternal perspective does change the way we look at life. Our values, goals, and resources are all looked at differently when we see life as a temporary tent. Ask learners to share how they responded to the final activity of Day 2 on pages 57-58. Make sure learners think hard about how they live. Do they live as if the grave is their final moment or do they live as if eternity is their final destiny?
6. Ask learners to summarize what Day 3 revealed concerning the "first motivating factor." After learners have identified the judgment of God as a key motivator, move to your next question: *How do you typically react when you hear the phrase "the fear of God"? What is your gut response?* Explain that we often have an incorrect view of God and fear of Him because we have been conditioned by our past. Some of us were raised in a fear-based understanding of God. Allow learners to react to this observation and share their stories. Read aloud 2 Corinthians 5:9-11. Ask: *How should we understand pleasing God and judgment based on this Scripture?* Refer to the final activity of Day 3 on page 60. Ask learners to share their thoughts and reactions.
7. Ask: *Looking at 2 Corinthians 5:12-15, what did Paul describe as the supreme motivator?* Help learners recognize that God's love made Paul willing to do courageous and risky things. For Paul, the love of Christ was all he needed! Ask learners to share their responses to the final activity of Day 4 on pages 61-62. Emphasize that we are always open and willing to serve the ones we love. God loves us; thus, He reconciles us through His Son. We can love God in return. To love God means wanting to please Him!
8. Explain that loving God is not an abstract phenomenon. Read aloud 2 Corinthians 5:16-17. Explain that the idea of being a "new creation" reveals that God, who is the Creator of all things, shapes us. Explain that the same amazing power that went into the origin of the universe is the same force that goes into our spiritual renewal. Ask: *Do you see yourself as a "new creation"? Explain why you feel the way you do.*
9. Ask learners to summarize the two motives described in Week 5—*the fear of God* and *the love of Christ.* Ask learners to look at the last activity of Day 5 on page 63. Encourage learners to share how they responded to the questions in this exercise.

The Glory of Ministry

What Everyone Needs to Hear

"All this is from God, who reconciled us to himself through Christ and gave us the ministry of reconciliation" (2 Cor. 5:18).

Once we truly understand and appreciate what Jesus Christ has done for us, it is impossible to keep it a secret! The wonderful story of new life in Christ absolutely shouts within us, demanding to be shared with others who still struggle with guilt, despair, shame, and hostility. Whenever we see another hurting human being, we know we have an opportunity for sharing. This is our ministry—an abundant ministry, available to all, as simple and as natural as breathing. The Apostle Paul describes this ministry in 2 Corinthians 5:18–6:2.

At first glance, how would you define the phrase "ministry of reconciliation"?

____

What specific ways do you visibly observe "alienation from God" affecting people around you?

____

Five times in this brief statement Paul stresses some form of the word *reconciliation.* Since people were designed to be indwelt by God, nothing could be more damaging to our humanity than to be estranged from the God who made us. Alienation from God is the fundamental sickness of humanity, and it breaks out in such hurtful expressions as guilt, hostility, despair, and even addiction.

How does Matthew 11:28 relate to your own experience with faith?

____

The best news humanity could ever hear is that some means of reconciliation with God has been found. It is the great privilege of Christians to declare this good news to those who desperately need it and who are willing to listen because of the hurts and holes in their own lives. Effective witness almost always begins at the point of need. "Come to me, all you who are weary and burdened," says Jesus, "and I will give you rest" (Matt. 11:28).

Nine elements of this ministry of reconciliation are underscored by Paul to indicate its greatness and its relevance. To review these nine elements is to become aware of the immense privilege of proclaiming such a message of reconciliation to hurting—and even hurtful—men and women.

The Ministry of Reconciliation, Part 1

The Ministry of Reconciliation Originates with God.

"All this is from God," says Paul. The offended one, God Himself, initiates the way of reconciliation. We, the offenders, only respond.

The good news does not originate with humans; it is not simply another way people have invented to find their own way back to God. The very nature of the good news is such that it couldn't have been invented by humans. It begins by postulating nothing in human beings except weakness, failure, and rebellion. By that one stroke, all competition is eliminated in the quest for salvation. No one can properly think of himself or herself as any closer to God than other people—apart from Christ. Those who pride themselves on their moral and respectable lives are no closer to God than the murderer or the sex pervert, for in reality, pride of respectability is just as much a manifestation of alienation from God as murder or debauchery.

This element of the good news irritates and offends many people. Those who count on their good works to save them are put off by this proclamation. They want God to take them on their terms. However, their offense is only further confirmation of the apostle's claim that "all this is from God." No flagrant sinner would dare dream he or she has some way to stand before God; no self-righteous person would imagine he or she needed anything to make himself or herself acceptable. The good news of reconciliation could never originate with humans. It comes wholly from God.

Do you like the idea of not having any power to initiate spiritual reconciliation? ____________

Why do you suppose it is hard for us to see God as the originator of reconciliation?

Why do we have a hard time accepting the idea that reconciliation "comes wholly from God"?

THE MINISTRY OF RECONCILIATION IS PERSONALLY EXPERIENCED.

The Christian who witnesses to the new covenant does not speak academically. He is able to identify fully with the hurt and darkness of those to whom he speaks, for he has (as the saying goes) "been there, done that" himself. But he has found something else, something so satisfying and complete as to make him eager to share it with others. He doesn't speak of "the plan of salvation" as though it were all theological doctrine, requiring only an intellectual grasp in order to receive it. Rather, he gives witness of a personal Lord who is at once the Savior and sustainer of his life. He does not convey the impression that when he surrendered to this Lord he was immediately and completely delivered from all struggle with evil, guilt, hate, and fear, but he makes it clear that the initial surrender produced a permanent change of heart. And power continually flows from that center to enable him to conquer—gradually, successively, day by day, step by step—the areas of his life yet dominated by evil and failure. He freely acknowledges his present failures but rejoices in the certainty that they too shall succumb to the authority and power of a resurrected Lord. As Paul wrote to the Romans, "Sin shall not be your master, because you are not under law, but under grace" (Rom. 6:14).

If you had only one sentence to describe your own experience with spiritual reconciliation, what would you say?

Where are the greatest battles in your spiritual life?

____

How does Romans 6:14 speak to your struggles?

____

The Ministry of Reconciliation, Part 2

THE MINISTRY OF RECONCILIATION IS UNIVERSALLY INCLUSIVE.

"[God] gave us the ministry of reconciliation. . . . God was reconciling the world to himself in Christ." One of the wonders of true Christianity is its universality. Though the church was originally Jewish, it was quickly embraced by the Gentiles. Christianity spread from the Holy Land into Europe and Africa, to Asia and the Americas. It has proven to satisfy the spiritual hunger of people from every culture and ethnic background, from every class—rich, poor, and in-between. Jesus is worshiped in the penthouses and in the ghettos, by those of the political right, left, and center. Men find that the message of Jesus speaks to their need as men, and women find that the message of Jesus fulfills and completes their femininity. It brings the wholeness of God to the whole need of every person—physically, spiritually, and emotionally.

What does "wholeness" look like in your life?

____

Do you personally feel a sense of "wholeness"? ________

Why did you answer as you did?

____

The silly idea has arisen somehow that Jesus and God the Father have different and opposing personalities. According to this idea, Jesus is tender and compassionate toward lost mankind and stands protectively between us and a vengeful, angry God the Father. Paul disposes of this faulty concept forever with his clear statement, "God was reconciling the world to himself in Christ." It was the Father who initiated the work of redemption. He gave His only Son, sending Him into the world to bring about our redemption and reconciliation through cruel death and subsequent resurrection. It was the Father who "did not spare his own Son, but gave him up for us all" (Rom. 8:32).

So it is the Father *and* the Son who, by means of the Spirit, reach out to a hurting, lonely world and offer pardon, peace, and joy to all who will come. No one is excluded by virtue of race, color, condition, or class. The door is wide open to all.

Think about two to three people in your life who are not yet followers of Jesus. How do you believe the universally relevant message of Jesus can speak effectively into their struggles and yearnings?

___

How about you? How has the message of reconciliation specifically brought pardon, peace, and joy into your life? ___

THE MINISTRY OF RECONCILIATION IS WITHOUT CONDEMNATION.

"Not counting men's sins against them." Because of the cross of Jesus, the problem human evil raises before God is totally eliminated. God does not require anything but the honest acknowledgment of evil to eliminate its degrading, destructive results in people's lives. No penance is demanded, nor will any be accepted. No self-chastisement is required. Any attempt to resort to these is but proof that the individual has not believed what God has plainly said. This is true not only when a person first comes to Christ, but it remains true throughout his or her entire life.

The penalty of death for any or all of my sins has already been fully borne by Christ—and that means death in all its varied forms. I bear my own sins when I refuse to believe God and seek in some way to justify them before God. But the experience of death ends the moment I believe Him: "Therefore, there is now no condemnation for those who are in Christ Jesus" (Rom. 8:1).

This is the element that especially makes reconciliation such good news. All God ever requires of us is that we acknowledge our evil and be willing to be delivered from its power. God accomplishes the actual *work* of deliverance for us on the basis of Jesus' death. The cross has *already* set us free; it is only waiting for us to believe it to become real in our experience.

What contributes to people's misunderstanding God, namely, thinking He is condemning?

____

How do 2 Corinthians 5:19 and Romans 8:1 address this?

____

Of course, certain natural consequences of our evil will still remain. Sin always leaves its scars. The person who repents from a lifestyle of sexual sin and turns to Christ will be forgiven—but forgiveness doesn't erase the natural consequences of that lifestyle such as broken relationships, emotional scars, or sexually transmitted diseases. The person who repents from a life of criminal behavior and turns to Christ will be forgiven—but forgiveness doesn't erase the possibility of punishment for those crimes and the need to make restitution. The consequences of old sins, even though forgiven, often remain. But those sins can no longer produce spiritual death in us because the resurrection life of Jesus now pulsates within us. The mistakes and rebellions of our past will be turned into instruments of grace to mellow and soften us and make us clearer and brighter manifestations of God's redeeming love.

How can your mistakes be used in a beneficial way, according to God's plan of reconciliation?

____

In the margin describe examples from your own experience

The Ministry of Reconciliation, Part 3

Why do you suppose God's wants to use us as His mouthpiece of reconciliation?

How does the word *incarnation* relate to our role as spokespersons for the gospel?

How are you specifically an instrument of reconciliation in the lives of those around you? Give examples in the space below.

The Ministry of Reconciliation Is Personally Delivered.

"He has committed to us the message of reconciliation." The good news does not come by means of angels. It is not announced from heaven by loud, impersonal voices. It doesn't even come by poring over dusty volumes from the past. In each generation it is delivered by living, breathing men and women who speak from their own experience. Incarnation, the word become flesh, is forever God's way of truly communicating with people. It comes always at the cost of hunger and thirst, personal hardship borne for Christ's sake—blood, sweat, and tears.

The Ministry of Reconciliation Is Authoritatively Accredited.

"We are therefore Christ's ambassadors, as though God were making his appeal through us." Ambassadors are the official spokesmen of a sovereign power in a foreign state. Their word is backed up by the power that sent them out—but only when the word of the ambassador truly represents the mind and will of the sending state. So Christians everywhere are authorized spokesmen for God, "God making his appeal through us," but only when they are living authentically as Christians. Whenever that is true, God honors their word by making visible and realistic changes in the lives of those who respond to their witness.

Do you typically feel like you carry the authority of God as His ambassador? Why or why not?

Do you feel timid or bold about representing Christ?

If more timid than bold, what contributes to feeling this way? ______________________________

If more bold than timid, what gives you this sense of confidence? ______________________________

THE MINISTRY OF RECONCILIATION IS VOLUNTARILY ACCEPTED.

"We implore you on Christ's behalf: Be reconciled to God." Throughout this passage the apostle uses words that underscore the noncoercive nature of the gospel: "appeal," "beseech," "entreat." Since we make our appeal "on behalf of Christ" or, literally, "in place of Christ," it is important that we be no more coercive than Jesus was when He ministered in the flesh on earth. In fact, authentic Christianity is Christ, by the Spirit, speaking through us today. It cannot be otherwise and still be of the Spirit. A remarkable absence of pressure characterizes the presentations Jesus made to people. He repeatedly offers Himself to them. He invites them to respond. He warns them of the consequences if they refuse. But He does not harangue them or use emotional stories to sway them. When they seem reluctant to respond, He neither prolongs the occasion nor makes the invitation easier. In fact, He is forever sending people away and thinning the ranks of His disciples.

What does it look like for you to be "appealing" to others regarding Christ? ______________________

When do you think we potentially cross the line into being coercive? ______________________________

When you think about the way faith was introduced to you, did you feel the healthy appeal of others or coercive force? ______________________

Appeal is made to the will to respond, and if it does not do so, the matter is left with God to work further in His will and time. This is true not only for the evangelist but also for the pastor-teacher or anyone who imparts the truth of the new covenant. "A man convinced against his will is of the same opinion still," says a wise old adage. Truth must find a willing response from the heart or it is of no value. Contrived responses are a waste of time.

The Ministry of Reconciliation, Part 4

What does it mean to you when Pastor Stedman says, "Evil was forever cut off from us in the cross"?

Doe your experience with Christianity exemplify a sense of release from sin? Why or why not?

In the space below, indicate the people and experiences that have contributed to the way you feel regarding evil's hold on your life.

The Ministry of Reconciliation Achieves the Impossible.

"God made him who had no sin to be sin for us, so that in him we might become the righteousness of God." Here is the supreme glory of the new covenant. It actually achieves what could never be achieved by fallen humans: righteousness (worth) before a holy God! It seems impossible even for God. How can a God of justice justify the unjust? How can a righteous God righteously declare a sinner to be righteous? It is a puzzle that staggers the angels. But it was achieved! He who knew no sin, Jesus the righteous one, was made (on the cross) to be *sin* on behalf of us, who knew no righteousness, in order that the righteousness of God might be forever *ours!*

Righteousness is not only our unchanging *standing* before a holy God; it is also our present *state* whenever we are walking in the Spirit. The cross, therefore, is forever the ground of Satan's defeat. It was the ace up God's sleeve that Satan could not have anticipated. The great accuser can never find any ground by which he can turn a righteous God against us, for *all* our evil was forever cut off from us in the cross, and we now have a totally new identity. We are one spirit with Jesus Himself.

The Ministry of Reconciliation Is Experienced Moment-by-Moment.

The opening verses of 2 Corinthians 6 continue the apostle's argument: "As God's fellow workers we urge you not to receive God's grace in vain. For he says, 'In the time of my favor I heard you, and in the day of salvation I helped you.' I tell you, now is the time of God's favor, now is the day of salvation" (vv. 1–2).

It is possible to accept the grace of God in vain. That is, it is possible to live much of life in dependence on the resources of the flesh rather than on the power and riches of the Spirit. Of course, for such moments or hours or days Christ has profited us nothing. We have Him, but we live as though He were not there. The grace and power of God are ours, but they do us no good.

Since we must take God's grace by faith (or dependence) and it comes to us moment-by-moment, then it is the present moment we must be concerned with. "I tell you, *now* is the time of God's favor, *now* is the day of salvation" (emphasis added). The fact that we walked in the Spirit a few moments ago is of no value to us now; the intention we have to walk in the Spirit in just a few more minutes does not redeem the present. If we choose to act in the flesh *now,* it is wasted time, gone forever, never to be retraced or regained. Let us run the race of life seeking to live each moment in the power and grace of the Spirit of Christ, for any time spent in the flesh is time in which we have accepted the grace of God in vain.

What do you think Paul meant when he said, "Now is the day of salvation"?

____

To what degree do the sentences at the left relate to your own life?

____

What is the benefit of living with the sense of immediacy that Paul described in 2 Corinthians 6:1-2?

____

This is the ministry of reconciliation that God has entrusted to us.

The Ministry of Reconciliation:

Originates with God, not humans;
Is personally experienced;
Is universally inclusive;
Is without condemnation;
Is delivered by people;
Is owned and accredited by God;
Is voluntarily accepted;
Achieves what otherwise is impossible; and
Is experienced moment-by-moment.

Review the nine elements listed to the left. Place a check mark (✓) next to those you feel you grasp. Place an "X" next to those you feel you struggle with.

Review the "Xs" and think about how you can increase in your life the truths in these categories to enhance your faith in Jesus.

God does not send us forth alone but goes with us Himself to be both the Author and the Finisher of our faith (see Heb. 12:2, KJV).

What a powerful and challenging opportunity His great ministry of reconciliation affords us! The Apostle Paul couldn't help being caught up with the glory and wonder of it—neither should you be able to!

NOTES

To the Leader:

Many Christians see a defined line between ministers and laity. Yet such a line doesn't exist in Scripture. We are all ministers and all have a defined ministry in this world. This lesson affords an opportunity to teach Christians that we all have a call to minister to those around us. Our ministry is well laid out in 2 Corinthians 5:18–6:2. See this lesson as an opportunity to renew people's vision and purpose for living!

Before the Session

Bring in a backpack or strong canvas sack filled with bricks.

During the Session

1. As learners come into class have each person give a try lifting the backpack or sack of bricks. (Make sure no one strains himself or herself.) Ask learners if they would like to carry such a sack around with them throughout one week's worth of daily routine. Explain that the sack of bricks is a visual way for us to understand the burden many people are carrying in life. It may not be weights, but it is certainly a load of other things—worries, sorrows, addiction, abuse, hurt, confusion, and so forth. Ask: *How can we be about helping people as they deal with their burdens?* Direct learners to read Matthew 11:28. Ask: *How does this verse relate to our burdens?*
2. Ask someone to read aloud 2 Corinthians 5:18–6:2. Explain that this passage will guide the remainder of today's discussion. Explain that we are called to be about the work of reconciliation as prescribed in this passage. Refer to the first activity in Day 1 on page 66. Encourage learners to share their thoughts on how they defined "ministry of reconciliation." Ask: *Have you been under the impression that your life should be devoted to a ministry of reconciliation? Why or why not?* Help learners recognize the false dividing line we have created between professional ministers and laity. Explain that this passage reveals there is no distinguishing line. We are all called to be ministers in the world. Ask: *How does it make you feel to know that God has called you to a ministry of reconciliation?*
3. Focus learners on 2 Corinthians 5:18. Ask: *What does it mean when Paul says, "all this is from God"? What are the implications of this statement regarding your part in a ministry of reconciliation?* Help learners to think about the fact that reconciliation is something initiated by God and not by our own efforts. Refer to the first activity under Day 2 on pages 67-68 to facilitate further discussion.
4. Ask: *What did the author mean by "the ministry of reconciliation is personally experienced"?* Lead learners to explore 2 Corinthians 5:18 for more

insight into how reconciliation is something we personally experience. We are not called to talk about something we know nothing about. We must be personally touched by God's reconciling love! Refer to Romans 6:14 for further understanding of the power of reconciliation that has touched our lives. Use the second activity of Day 2 on page 68 as a way to discuss the personal touch of God's reconciliation.

5. Ask: *What insight does 2 Corinthians 5:19 offer as far as the nature of Christ's reconciliation?* Explain that Christ's reconciliation is not for a limited number of people. The message of the gospel relates to all people no matter their ethnicity, gender, social class, and so forth. Emphasize that Jesus brings wholeness. Refer to the activity on page 70 for further discussion. Ask learners to share ideas how the message of Jesus will specifically address the unique needs of their friends who are not yet believers.
6. Have someone read aloud Romans 8:1. Ask: *Does the message of this verse match up with your own experience regarding Christianity? Why or why not? How many of your friends and family members are nervous about church because they think it is a place where they will be condemned? Why do you suppose people feel this way?* Encourage learners to refer to the activity on the top of page 71 as they discuss the above questions. In particular help learners discover that Jesus did not come to condemn the world. (Reference John 3:16-17 to further emphasize this point.) And assure learners that our own sin and mistakes can be transformed into instruments of grace to help others who are estranged from God. Ask learners to share their responses to the activity on the bottom of page 71.
7. Ask: *With regard to 2 Corinthians 5:20, what does it mean that we are considered "Christ's ambassadors"?* Emphasize that being an ambassador suggests we are authorized agents of God on earth. Encourage learners to share what it means to be an ambassador based on what they read under Day 4. Ask learners to share how they responded to the activity on pages 72-73. Ask: *Based on 2 Corinthians 5:20, what does it mean for you to be an ambassador?* Refer to Pastor Stedman's discussion of how our job as an ambassador has everything to do with "appealing" to others. Use the activity on the bottom of page 73 to help learners grasp their role as one who appeals to others with the message of the gospel.
8. Allow learners to reread 2 Corinthians 5:21–6:2. Ask: *Do any of those you know, who have yet to embrace Christ, seem to have a strong unwillingness when it comes to embracing the gospel?* **Continued in the margin.**

What will it take to help such people come to saving faith? Point learners to how 2 Corinthians 5:21 gives hope. Direct learners to think about the meaning of 2 Corinthians 6:1-2. Explain that we must look at our ministry of reconciliation with a sense of immediacy. Ask learners to share their responses to the activity on page 75.

9. Conclude by reviewing the 9 elements of reconciliation listed on page 75. Ask learners to share how they responded to the final activity in the margin on page 75.

Exhibit A

day One

Ways to Commend the New Covenant

The new covenant cannot be lived in isolation but must bring us into contact with others, both Christians and non-Christians because *authentic Christianity is designed for the world as it is.* Therefore, the apostle says: "We put no stumbling block in anyone's path, so that our ministry will not be discredited. Rather, as servants of God we commend ourselves in every way" (2 Cor. 6:3–4).

Then Paul presents a most remarkable list of very practical ways by which the new covenant may be commended to others in verses 4–8.

We shall look now at this impressive list to discover the right way Christians can commend themselves and the teaching of the new covenant to others.

The translators have obscured, in part, the divisions the apostle indicates in this paragraph. There are three major groupings of thought:

In great endurance:

in troubles,
in hardships,
in distresses;

in beatings,
in imprisonments,
in riots;
in hard work,
in sleepless nights
in hunger;

By means of:

purity,
understanding,
patience,
kindness;

the Holy Spirit,
sincere love,
truthful speech,
the power of God;

With the weapons of righteousness:

in the right hand and the left,
in glory and dishonor,
in bad report and good report.

Which of the adverse pressures listed seem most familiar to your own experience in life?

____

____

Which of the character points listed feel familiar to you?

____

____

Which ones feel foreign?

____

____

It is obvious that the first group deals with the adverse pressures a Christian can encounter in life. The second group describes the character that must be displayed in the midst of these pressures. And the third group deals with the results produced, both good and apparently evil.

Paul fully exemplifies all these things! The apostles were pattern Christians, chosen to experience the full range of pressures and possibilities so that we might have in them (and supremely in the Lord Jesus) an example to follow. It is not likely we will be called on to endure *all* these experiences, but we will surely be asked to endure *some* of them. Let us remember that the world around is watching us and only the manifestation of what Paul lists here will commend us to those who are watching our lives.

Paul certainly doesn't guarantee that life will always go smoothly. Are you OK if things don't go so well for you despite the fact that you pursue God's righteousness? __________

Why bother following Christ if things could go bad, as described in 2 Corinthians 6:7-10?

____

Who in your life do you believe is watching you closely to see how you react as a Christian?

____

How does it make you feel to know people are watching you?

____

Endurance That Endures

The key word to the first group is *endurance.* It means far more than simply toughing it out. Even non-Christians can endure hardness in that sense and some take great pride in their ability to do so.

The Greek word used here, *hupomone,* goes far beyond that. Rather, it is the courageous triumph that takes all the pressure and emerges with a cheer! It not only refuses to be broken by the pressure but is actually grateful for the opportunity to endure, knowing it will bring glory to God.

Paul triumphantly endured everything on his list, often repeatedly. There were *afflictions* or, literally, "distresses." There were pressures that bore heavily upon his spirit—cares and intense anxieties that seldom let up in his life. There were *hardships*—the inescapable discomforts of life. And there were *calamities,* or to be more exact, "strictures," narrow places that seem to close one in on every side, offering no escape. In each of these circumstances the triumphant endurance produced by the new covenant commends Paul to those who are watching his life.

Next, there were troubles that stemmed directly from human opposition. There were *beatings* or *stripes.* Further on in this letter Paul says, "Five times I received from the Jews the forty lashes minus one. Three times I was beaten with rods, once I was stoned" (11:24–25). These painful beatings left their scars on him so that he could write to the Galatians, "Finally, let no one cause me trouble, for I bear on my body the marks of Jesus" (Gal. 6:17).

Often accompanying the beatings were *imprisonments.* Clement of Rome tells us the apostle was put into prison seven times, though only four of these are recorded in the Scriptures. At least two imprisonments were for more than two years, so Paul spent at least five years in prison and perhaps much more.

But that was not all. There were also *tumults.* This is a reference to the riots and mob violence that he sometimes provoked by the sweeping social changes his preaching produced. Perhaps nothing is more frightening than an angry mob, out of control, bent upon venting its rage on some hapless victim. But God enabled Paul to endure all of these encounters and trials with triumphant courage.

The last category of events calling for endurance involved, first, the *labors* he assumed. The word he uses here describes hard, unremitting toil, to the point of exhaustion. Paul doubtless spent many long hours at his tentmaking so he could present the gospel without charge! There were also *watchings*—sleepless nights, spent in prayer and meditation. These were not a matter of mere convenience to Paul but required grace and commitment. Then there was *hunger.* The reference is probably to periods of fasting, some deliberately chosen and some enforced on him by the circumstances in which he found himself. These would take their toll of his physical and emotional strength, but through them all he was enabled to endure triumphantly.

What words would you use to describe the hardships you've endured because of your faith?

____

How have hardships affected your faith?

____

If you were to give someone else advice on how he or she can endure hard times, what would your tips be?

____

The Secret Described

What was the secret of such endurance? It was never by a clenching of his fists, a jutting of his jaw, and a determination of his will to show the world how much he could take for Christ.

What have you typically done to endure hardships? How have you coped with difficult situations?

____

Were your efforts to endure hardship as more about your stamina or about God's strength? Explain your response.

____

____

Paul possessed a certain kind of character that saw him through his troubles. It had to be invariable, or nearly so, for he never knew when it would be required. It consisted of four elements. First, there was *purity.* This refers to the careful avoidance of all sin that defiles or stains the flesh or spirit. Paul never allowed himself to be found in a compromising relationship with anyone. He carefully guarded not only his behavior but his thought life, for he knew that is where defilement begins. Whenever he found himself toying with impurity, he immediately brought it to the Lord Jesus and obtained His cleansing and forgiveness.

Why is purity an important foundation in one's own character?

____

Next there was *knowledge.* His mind was deliberately set on truth, as he had learned it from the Scriptures and revelations of the Lord. He judged all persons and events, not from a human point of view but from the divine viewpoint as revealed by the Spirit. Scripture was always his guide.

How would you rate your level of Scripture knowledge? (Use the scale below to answer this question.)

Poor **Excellent**

How often do you rely on Scripture to help you discern what to do?

Rarely **Often**

Describe specific examples in your past when Scripture aided you in your effort to endure hard times.

Third came *forbearance.* The Greek word, *macrothumia,* means "patience," especially with regard to people. By nature Paul was impatient and hard driving. But he learned by the Spirit to wait for others to catch up, to be understanding about their weaknesses, and to wait quietly for the Lord to do the work of correction that was needed, for "to his own master he stands or falls" (Rom. 14:4).

How can patience benefit you when you are dealing with adverse pressures?

Finally, there was *kindness.* The original word has been described as meaning "the sympathetic kindliness or sweetness of temper that puts others at their ease and shrinks from giving pain."

These four marks of Paul's character were what enabled him to endure.

Does your effort to spiritually endure hard times typically bring out the best or the worst in you?

____

How can the quality of kindness guide our efforts to endure hard times?

____

Deeper Yet

But there was something deeper even than these. The four characteristics of purity, knowledge, forbearance, and kindness were visible to other people. They lay in the realm of Paul's soul, his conscious experience in life. Deeper still, in the depths of his spirit, were the forces that undergirded and kept on making possible the display of the four characteristics just listed.

Behind everything else and at the root of it all was "the Holy Spirit." The third person of the Godhead is the gift of both the Father and the Son, serving as the guarantee of all else to come, dwelling permanently in Paul's heart, was the uncreated source of all that sustained Paul. It was the Spirit's constant delight to release to Paul at all times "the life of Jesus." Jesus Himself, by the Spirit, lived in Paul and upheld and empowered him, just as He lives in us and upholds us and empowers us through all our trials and tribulations. That "life of Jesus" invariably consists of three elements: love, truth, and power. This "life of Jesus" was continually supplied to Paul through the Spirit, explaining all that He was and did. This was the "sincere love," "truthful speech," and "the power of God" Paul talked about. No wonder he could handle life the way he did!

How have you seen the Holy Spirit manifest in your life?

____

Do you feel the Holy Spirit fills you with the qualities Paul mentioned in 2 Corinthians 6:6-7? ______

Do any of these qualities seem lacking in your life? ___ If so, which ones?

____

But Paul isn't through yet. Though the new covenant is designed to make us strong, it equips us *so that we might affect others.* There is always that watching world before which we must be commended! So Paul's final category speaks of the effect of "the weapons of righteousness." He sees the worth and value he has in God's eyes—worth and value that is based on the righteousness of Christ, not any righteousness of his own—as a kind of sword or spear by which we attack the forces of darkness. With these weapons, we set free those who have been held in bondage by Satan. Hence, the term "weapons of righteousness." *Righteousness,* here, is a summary term gathering up the four distinctives Paul listed in the previous section: purity, understanding, patience, and kindness. These four "weapons of righteousness" have a powerful effect on others in two ways:

First, such righteousness affects both "the right hand and the left." By this Paul refers to the public and private life. The right hand is the public life, the left hand is the private. Thus, the effect of a righteous life will touch both the public actions of others (their social relationships) and their private lives as well (changing their attitudes). True Christianity does not make superficial changes—it changes people within and without.

In your own life, which seems more affected by God's righteousness—your public or your private life? Why?

____

If you enjoyed these studies from Ray Stedman and desire to purchase your own copy of his book *Authentic Christianity* to read and study in greater detail, visit the LifeWay Christian Store serving you. Or you can order a copy by calling 1-800-233-1123.

My Action Steps:

1.

2.

3.

4.

5.

6.

7.

Second, the effect of such change is also twofold: "in honor and dishonor." Those freed by Christ will be placed in varying positions before the world. Some will occupy positions of honor, others will be obscure men and women about whom the world knows or cares nothing. But even these will find a varying acceptance. Some will be of "bad report" and others will be of "good report." But, whether honored by the world or dishonored, whether held in good or bad esteem, all are equally loved and owned by God, all are equally empowered by the Spirit (if they choose to draw on Him), and all are expected to live before the world in such a way as to commend the gospel to all people.

Are you going to be OK and satisfied if you are rejected by the world "yet loved and owned by God"?
❑ Yes ❑ No ❑ I'm not sure

Is the following true or false for you? God's love is enough to give me what I need in life. ___________

Does the pattern of your life agree with your answer to the above question? Give examples in the margin.

The Paradoxical Christian

Paul describes a series of magnificent paradoxes in his depiction of the authentic Christian in 2 Corinthians 6:8–10. He says that he and his fellow authentic Christians are "genuine, yet regarded as impostors; known, yet regarded as unknown; dying, and yet we live on; beaten, and yet not killed; sorrowful, yet always rejoicing; poor, yet making many rich; having nothing, and yet possessing everything."

Clearly, authentic Christians present an enigma to the world because their lives consist of a series of paradoxes. Only the man or woman who stands poised between two worlds can qualify for such a description. The authentic Christian is in a highly vulnerable position, stretched between God and man. We must be content to be called imposters by some, to be thought of as unknown, to be threatened and punished, to be poor and have nothing—all the while knowing that, before God, the very reverse is true! As God sees us, we are his true children, known to all heaven, living and rejoicing in the spirit when the flesh is perishing, ever imparting the unsearchable riches of Christ to many, and being heirs of all creation when time trembles into eternity.

How does it make you feel to be misunderstood as a Christian?

Is it not fitting that the apostle should close this great discourse with an earnest appeal, rising out of the depths of his heart in verses 11–13?

Review 2 Corinthians 6:8-11. Which of the paradoxes mentioned seems closest to your own experience?

Love, truth, and power all require response to be fully operative. Each will grow to infinite expansion if it is met by faith, though it be as small as a grain of mustard seed. Paul was not holding anything back from the Corinthians. He had opened his heart to them and told them everything he had learned from the Lord. Their present weakness was due to only one thing—a failure to respond to the truth they knew, a reluctance to act on what they had been told. So his appeal comes as a father to his children: "Open wide your hearts!"

I invite you to bow your knees before the Father of our Lord Jesus Christ, and in His name, pray: "Father, make me a qualified minister of the new covenant. Open my eyes to the full meaning of the truth that Jesus lives in me, by the Spirit. Make me hunger and thirst after His righteousness, so that according to your promise I might be filled. Amen."

How open is the condition of your own heart when it comes to submitting to the challenge of authentic Christianity?

What in these seven lessons did you feel yourself most resistant to hearing?

Return to the things that rubbed you the wrong way and ask God to open your heart to consider what it would take to make you an authentic Christian.

What makes you want to hold back instead of being open?

Develop an action plan related to these lessons. Write these action steps in the margin on page 86. Review the action steps often and reflect on your progress. Allow these steps to serve as a means of putting into practice in your life Paul's teaching in 2 Corinthians 2:14–6:13.

NOTES

To the Leader:

Christianity seems good on paper. Yet, when the winds of trouble rush upon life, is the Christian faith tough enough to stick it out? The amazing news is that followers of Jesus can stick it out through God's power. Living an authentic faith is tough and requires endurance. Challenge learners with this final lesson. Use this lesson to encourage learners to stay true to their faith, especially when hardships come!

Before the Session

Bring a pressure cooker.

During the Session

1. Read dramatically 2 Corinthians 6:3-13. Explain that this passage will serve as the focus of the remainder of your discussion. Ask: *As we read through this passage and as you reflect on what you studied in this seven-week series, what caught your attention?*
2. Ask: *What did you think about Paul's list of hardships in 2 Corinthians 6:3-6?* Explain that Paul experienced plenty of moments when he was feeling the pressure of his hardships. Place the pressure cooker in front of learners. Give enough details about how a pressure cooker works so people fully understand the pressure generated by this device. Explain that Paul's authentic faith was definitely put to the test in the pressure cooker of his circumstances. Ask: *What kind of pressure cooker moments have you faced in life? How have such experiences affected your outlook on faith?* Discuss the activity in Day 1 on pages 79-80.
3. Ask: *With regard to Paul's list in 2 Corinthians 6:4-5, describe a season of your life when you've felt like endurance was the key to survival as a Christian.* Call attention to the activity at the end of Day 2 on page 81. Ask learners to share their responses.
4. Ask: *With reference to Day 3, what was Paul's secret to having tenacious endurance? How did Paul's strategy match up with your own methods for enduring hardship?* Refer to all Day 3 activities to facilitate further discussion about the keys to developing a sense of God-empowered endurance. Many of the activities in Day 3 are diagnostic, meaning they help learners evaluate how they live with regard to the character elements mentioned. Take your time working through this section and allow learners plenty of time to think through where they are strong and where they struggle.
5. Reread aloud 2 Corinthians 6:6-7. Ask: *What were the deeper forces that drove Paul as he lived out his faith?* Focus learners on the deeper forces mentioned in the Scripture passage—the Holy Spirit, love, truth,

and the power of God. Focus particularly on the Holy Spirit. Refer to the activity on the top of page 85. Remember that the Holy Spirit is God with us in Spirit. We often neglect speaking about the Holy Spirit, so it will be helpful for learners to allow them to spend time sharing their own experiences regarding the Holy Spirit.

NOTES

6. Ask: *With regard to 2 Corinthians 6:7-8, how would you explain the meaning of "weapons of righteousness"?* Encourage learners to review both the Scripture text and Pastor Stedman's material in Day 4. Share with learners that this phrase ultimately relates to the four character elements mentioned of purity, understanding, patience, and kindness. Review with learners how these weapons of righteousness affect us. Utilize the remaining activities of Day 4 on pages 85-86 to facilitate discussion regarding the impact of God's righteousness on our lives as Christians.
7. Read the following quotation from Pastor Stedman: "Clearly, authentic Christians present an enigma to the world because their lives consist of a series of paradoxes." Ask learners to explain what they think this means. Ask: *Of the paradoxes mentioned in 2 Corinthians 6:8-10, which feel closest to your own experiences as a Christian?*
8. Conclude your discussion by reading aloud 2 Corinthians 6:11-13. Explain that this is Paul's earnest appeal to us that we would be open to God. Explain that authentic Christianity will not happen unless we allow ourselves to be open. Ask learners to share how they answered the interactive activity in the lower portion of the margin on page 87. Be sure to ask aloud each of the questions printed in the margin. *[How open is the condition of your own heart when it comes to submitting to the challenge of authentic Christianity? What makes you want to hold back instead of being open?]*
9. In conclusion, ask learners to share their responses to the concluding activity of Day 5 on the bottom of page 87. This activity encourages the creation of action steps. Encourage learners to discuss their actions steps, or if they did not create their action steps, help learners develop their action plan in class. After everyone has had an opportunity to share his or her steps, allow time for learners to pray for one another. Particularly pray for all learners to have a commitment to follow through with the action steps they shared as well as a commitment to seek an authentic Christian lifestyle in their daily lives.

ABOUT THE WRITERS

Beth Moore

has written numerous books and Bible studies that have been read by women of all ages, races, and denominations. Beth's Living Proof Live conferences have been attended by more than 421,000 women.

Beth's ministry is grounded in and fueled by her service at her home fellowship, Houston's First Baptist Church, where she teaches a 700-member Sunday School class. Beth and her husband, Keith, have been married over 26 years and have two adult daughters, Amanda and Melissa. The Moores live in Houston, Texas, with their two dogs, Beanie and Sunny.

AMY SUMMERS wrote the teaching plans for these lessons. Amy is an experienced writer for LifeWay Bible study curriculum, a wife, a mother, and a Sunday School leader from Arden, North Carolina. She is a graduate of Baylor University and Southwestern Baptist Theological Seminary.

ABOUT THIS STUDY

We see it reported in the headlines, confessed in the pulpits, and hidden in the pews in churches around the world. The seduction of God's people by the deceiver is a tale as old as the garden, but we are always surprised when it happens. Satan is a lion on the prowl and we are his prey.

Why do you think Satan may be more active today in attacking Christians than ever before?

WE ARE CLOSE TO THE END

Before you begin this study spend some time in prayer, asking the Lord to show you how you can best protect yourself from the traps of Satan.

When Godly People Do Ungodly Things

Satan has a strategy for destroying the testimony of Christians, and we must arm ourselves against his attacks. He hates being exposed as the fraud he is and that's one of the chief goals of these lessons. My specific prayer for this message is threefold:

- that God will use the pages of this study to shed light on Satan's massive campaign, in our current and future generations, to seduce the saints.
- that God will use this message to remind a battered and bruised believer how loved he is and how much the Father longs for his complete restoration. We have never gone so far that we can't come home.
- that many readers will wise up to Satan's seductive schemes and fortify their lives before he traps them into something ungodly.

This study is written in three parts. Weeks 1 and 2 are the warning, both biblical and experiential, that Satan is heightening his attack on those who are devout believers in Jesus Christ. Weeks 3 and 4 comprise ways we can fortify ourselves against Satan's full-scale attack on the lives of the elect in the latter days. Weeks 5 and 6 are the road home for the one who has been deceived and seduced by the enemy into a season of ungodliness.

I pray you will see this journey to its completion.

Beth Moore

The Warning

Prime Targets

"I am afraid that just as Eve was deceived by the serpent's cunning, your minds may somehow be led astray from your sincere and pure devotion to Christ" (2 Cor. 11:3).

I am terrified by the letters I receive from believers who loved God and walked with Him faithfully for years then found themselves suddenly overtaken by a tidal wave of temptation and unholy assault. Many believers are convinced such things can't happen. They are wrong.

Accounts of formerly pure lives suddenly knee-deep in the mire are absolutely authentic. Not one of them presents him- or herself as an innocent victim. They are horrified and taken aback at what they have done and what they appear capable of doing. Over and over I've heard renditions of the statement, "For the life of me, I can't figure out how something like this could have happened."

Wholehearted. Sincere. Pure devotion to Christ. That very kind of person can be beguiled by the enemy, whose utmost fantasy is to corrupt and seduce the real thing. Unsettling, isn't it?

"If any person is overtaken in misconduct or sin of any sort, you who are spiritual [who are responsive to and controlled by the Spirit] should set him right and restore and reinstate him, without any sense of superiority and with all gentleness, keeping an attentive eye on yourself, lest you should be tempted also" (Gal. 6:1, AMP).

Read Galatians 6:1 in the margin. Underline the words that describe those who are spiritual. Circle the danger.

Even the one who is spiritual can be tempted by the same sins that have overtaken another. The casualties are growing in number by harrowing leaps and bounds. Many just aren't talking because they are scared. Not so much of God as they are of the church. To say that the body of Christ would be shocked to know how bloody and bruised by defeat we are is a gross understatement. The better news is that God is not shocked. Grieved perhaps, but not shocked. He told us this was coming.

Read 2 Thessalonians 2:7-8. Who will be revealed when Jesus returns? 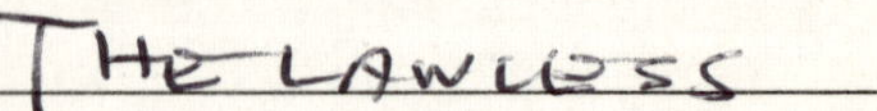

If the Apostle Paul could testify in his generation that "the secret power of lawlessness is already at work" (2 Thess. 2:7), who can begin to estimate the acceleration that has taken place over the last two thousand years?

Jesus warned His followers of a time of "great distress, unequaled from the beginning of the world until now" (Matt. 24:21).

Read Matthew 24:9-12. What five warnings did Jesus give His disciples? Write them in the margin.

1. PERSECUTED
PUT TO DEATH
2. HATED
TURNED AWAY
3. FALSE PROPHETS
DECEIVED
4. INCREASE OF
WICKEDNESS
5. LOVE WILL
GROW COLD

These warnings have applied to all ages, but many Bible scholars believe they point specifically to the war going on in our present and near future.

We want to understand how godly people can do ungodly things. Then we want to search out biblical remedies. So what does the approach of the end have to do with godly people falling before a satanic assault? Everything!

I believe Satan has two primary motivations: (1) to exact revenge on God by wreaking havoc on His children and (2) to try to incapacitate the believer's God-given ability to overcome him.

The more we understand the covering of Christ's blood, the more we overcome a foe who is otherwise far too strong for us. Satan is out to destroy the testimony of the believer. The more influential the testimony, the better.

What does 1 Peter 5:8 say Satan seeks to do?

PROWLS AROUND LIKE A ROARING LION

What was Peter's advice in 1 Peter 5:9? RESIST, STAND FIRM

The final word in verse 9 is *sufferings*. Not everyone in a stronghold of sin is having a good time. Many people wrongly assume that all departures from godliness are nothing but defiance, rebellion, and proofs of inauthenticity. They have no idea of the suffering involved when someone with a genuine heart for God slips from the path.

Increasing numbers of brothers and sisters are undergoing tremendous suffering at the paws of the roaring lion. Some of it comes in an unexpected, overwhelming season of temptation. The temptations can vary in type, but one thing is for sure: They are tailor-made to catch the believer off guard. Many sincere believers fall before they even know what hit them.

Background on Satan

Many believers think Satan is parallel to or as powerful as God. Let's be very careful not to give Satan more credit than he is due. While he is tremendously potent, armed, and dangerous, he is not the equal of the Most High God.

That doesn't mean the evil one is not a threat. Only the Almighty Three-in-One can overpower Satan. We walk in the victory Christ won for us only when we are "strong in the Lord and in his mighty power" (Eph. 6:10).

"Now is the time for judgment on this world; now the prince of this world will be driven out" (John 12:31).

"The prince of this world now stands condemned" (John 16:11).

"I saw Satan fall like lightning from heaven" (Luke 10:18).

How did Jesus refer to Satan in John 12:31 and 16:11?

PRINCE OF THIS EARTH WORLD

What does Luke 10:18 suggest about Satan's present power? LIKE A LIGHTING

So why is a defeated enemy so hard at work in a post-Calvary world? Perhaps this illustration will help.

In the United States our presidential elections occur in November, but the new president does not assume his position until January. Let's see if I can explain the parallel. I am convinced Scripture teaches that Christ Jesus will visibly return to earth and rule in righteousness for a thousand years. I also believe the "scroll" described in Revelation 5 is somewhat of a title deed to the world system. God permitted that authority to fall into Satan's hands for a time, after man's forced exodus from the garden. One day God will place that title deed back in the hands of its rightful ruler. At that time, Christ will return to earth, conquer every foe, and take His seat of authority.

We live in the period leading up to Christ taking His rightful throne. Christ is already Lord of lords and King of kings, but His kingdom is currently not of this world (see John 18:36). The day is coming when the nature of the kingdom will change. The Christ who reigns today in believers will reign outwardly and absolutely. He will take back what the enemy has stolen.

What political term does the illustration suggest could be applied to Satan?
❑ Favorite son ☒ Lame duck ❑ Front runner ❑ Shoe in

Not only is Satan a lame duck but his time is short. Peter described the consummation of the age in 2 Peter 3:10,12-13. Read these verses printed in the margin. Don't miss the significance of Peter's words from Satan's perspective. All beings will be in their eternal state from this time forward—whether redeemed in the presence of God or unredeemed in "the lake of fire" (Rev. 20:15).

The thought of the future of the unredeemed makes me shiver. I have no desire for anyone to go there. Not even the vilest sinner. I pray for all to repent! If God was willing to save me, He is willing to save anyone who asks.

"The heavens will disappear with a roar; the elements will be destroyed by fire, and the earth and everything in it will be laid bare. … That day will bring about the destruction of the heavens by fire, and the elements will melt in the heat. But in keeping with his promise we are looking forward to a new heaven and a new earth, the home of righteousness" (2 Pet. 3:10,12-13).

What does the Lord desire according to 2 Peter 3:9?

___

Election day took place on the cross. Christ has the only valid claim as the ultimate ruler of all creation. That's why the Apostle John saw "a Lamb, looking as if it had been slain, standing in the center of the throne, encircled by the four living creatures and the elders. … He came and took the scroll from the right hand of him who sat on the throne" (Rev. 5:6-7).

The one on the throne is God, of course. He is the all-powerful, ultimate ruler of heaven and earth, and nothing happens except by His perfect or permissive will. Yes, Satan has been "prince of this world," but only by divine permissive will and to accomplish God's own purposes. Satan was completely defeated by the offering of the perfect, sinless life of the Son of God on the cross. One day Christ will assume full reign of the world system where Satan has wreaked such havoc. Presently, however, the world exists in the period between the new election and the earthly inauguration of Christ.

Christ's kingdom is here now and will also be in the future. The archdemon knows his time of trying to undermine it is coming to a close, so he furiously unleashes his power to the full extent of God's permissive will. The dragon is in a tailspin, and he is whipping everything he can in the time he has left. Because his ultimate fury is at God, nothing gives Satan greater unholy pleasure than assaulting God's children.

Our purpose through this study, then, is to understand how the people described in 2 Corinthians 11:2-3 as being wholeheartedly, sincerely, and purely devoted to Christ can be beguiled by Satan and have their minds corrupted and seduced.

Certainly no one will argue that a believer can be characterized as godly while practicing ungodly things. Our task is to understand how a person who has consistently walked with God can be so powerfully seduced to ungodliness.

Has today's lesson given you insight into who Satan is?
❑ Yes ❑ No If so, summarize your insight in the margin.

Sexually Oriented Bondage

"Flee from sexual immorality. All other sins a man commits are outside his body, but he who sins sexually sins against his own body" (1 Cor. 6:18).

All seduction is not sexually oriented. Believers can be seduced by power, money, position, false doctrine, or by any number of flesh-fueling pumps.

However, Satan so vehemently despises what Christ has done for mortals that one of his chief objectives is to make the clean feel unclean. He desires to stain the beautiful bride of Christ. Satan can't *make* the bride do anything, so he does everything he can to *get* her to.

The nature of humankind is to act out of how we feel rather than what we know. One of our most important defenses against satanic influence is learning to behave out of what we know is truth rather than what we feel.

One of our most important defenses against satanic influence is learning to behave out of what we know is truth rather than what we feel.

If we have received Christ as our Savior, Satan is forced to work from the outside. Thus he manipulates outside influences to affect the inside decision-makers of the heart and mind.

Few things accomplish Satan's goal of inducing feelings and actions of uncleanness in those who are clean like sexual seduction. Somehow Satan makes sure it seems dirtier than the rest of the dirt. He also likes to instigate falls that carry long-term effects. God forgives sin the moment we repent, but its ramifications can take longer to heal.

Sexual sin is a perfect choice to achieve his goals. It can be highly addictive. It breeds shame like nothing else and has horrendous ramifications.

Based on 1 Corinthians 6:18-20, why is sexual sin a perfect choice to achieve Satan's goals?

____

Stealing, like all sin, is serious and carries lasting consequences of violating God's law. Yet if I stole money and then dumped it in the garbage, in some respects I could walk away without taking the sin with me. However, if I commit sexual sin, I have a much harder time dumping the garbage. Why? The sin was against my own body and wields much stronger staying power.

Only Christ through the power of His cross can peel off the adhesive effects of sexual sin. The sin is forgiven the moment the person repents, but healing can take longer. We must learn to trust God with our sexuality. Surely it's more than coincidental that Satan is having his greatest field day over the very dimension of our lives that we are most reluctant to bring before God for help, healing, and wholeness.

Seduction can take many forms, but Satan is having a field day by sexually seducing saints. Do you see what he has done through E-porn? Pastors and lay leaders who never bought an illicit magazine are suddenly falling under a wave of temptation to look "just once" at a pornographic Web site.

More often than not, "just once" turns into "just twice." Then three times, four times, and a believer who once walked with God in purity has developed the fiercest addiction of his or her entire life. Everything is affected. The marriage. The children. The workplace. The ministry.

Have you or someone you know been affected by pornography? ❑ Yes ❑ No What were the ramifications?

____

Satan already knew that. It went exactly as he planned. It doesn't have to keep going his way, though. His ultimate goal is that people follow the seducing spirits so far that they "turn away from the faith" (1 Tim. 4:1, AMP). If you have been powerfully seduced into the demonic doctrine of sexual perversion, don't turn away from the faith! Turn back!

Satan will do everything he can to hang on once he gets a foothold in our lives. The longer we wait to cry out for deliverance and to cooperate with

God, the tighter the grip grows on the yoke. If Satan has you in chains and you want out, hang in there! The last part of our study is dedicated to your full return and the return of others, no matter what the yoke.

As you close your study today, would you be willing to pray the following prayer with me? Personalize the prayer by using the pronouns *me, I,* and *my*.

God, help us. We are under attack. Far too many believers who have histories of faithfulness with You are falling for the Devil's schemes. Please open our eyes and show us the way! Hear the desperate cries of Your children.

Common Claims of the Seduced

"We do not have a high priest who is unable to sympathize with our weaknesses, but we have one who has been tempted in every way, just as we are—yet was without sin. Let us then approach the throne of grace with confidence, so that we may receive mercy and find grace to help us in our time of need" (Heb. 4:15-16).

I explained earlier how my concern grew out of reading unnerving testimonials from people who had devoted their lives to Christ and walked with God consistently for an extended period of time only to be suddenly seduced into ungodly behavior.

I have since met with a substantial number of them face-to-face, not as a counselor but as a researcher. I asked some hard questions and got what I believe were some very honest answers.

By no means do I suggest that all seductions share these commonalities. We have no idea how many shapes, sizes, and forms seductions can take. I have been shocked, however, by a number of common claims that I think are worth our notice. Those who were enticed to do ungodly things after living godly lives shared many of the following 16 claims. We will look at them over the next two days.

"If someone is caught in a sin, you who are spiritual should restore him gently. But watch yourself, or you also may be tempted" (Gal. 6:1).

Common Claims

1. *Individuals were caught off guard by a sudden onslaught of temptation or attack.* Not one planned his or her season of ungodliness. Many described having already sinned before they even knew what hit them. Sound impossible? Read Galatians 6:1 printed in the margin.

After catching his prey off guard, the enemy does all he can to make the victim feel completely trapped; but, as we'll discover, he can't keep up the facade indefinitely.

2. *The season of overwhelming temptation and seduction often followed huge spiritual markers with God.* These godly people who then did ungodly things were not walking in sin when the wave of seduction hit.

Christ Himself endured a dreadful time of testing after receiving great blessing. Of course, Jesus endured His season of temptation without sin, but the experience was inconceivably brutal. Knowing all that would come upon us, our faithful God made every provision, even in our temptation.

3. *Everyone described a mental bombardment.* Another way to describe the same thing is obsessive thinking. This one isn't hard to understand. It is one of the clearest signs of a fierce demonic stronghold. Second Corinthians 11:2-3 states that believers can be devoted to Christ with their whole heart, yet Satan can corrupt and seduce their minds.

The very nature of a stronghold is that something is exalted in our minds contrary to the knowledge of God. Breaking free from these mentally obsessive strongholds always requires bringing those previously exalted imaginations into the captivity of Christ's authority. We have divine power to demolish strongholds.

4. *Many caught in relational seductions testified Satan got to them through someone close.* The nature of seduction implies an unexpected, well-disguised lure. Satan looks for ways he can get close to the godly and gain trust.

Not everyone who appears trustworthy is. Perhaps we've all had times when we weren't terribly trustworthy ourselves. We should be desperate for discernment. Thankfully, God is willing to supply it. Part of our fortification against seduction will be making sure a door in our lives has not been opened through unhealthy relationships.

5. *Many testified to early warning signals.* I asked, "Did you ever get a flag of some kind that caused you to think you ought not proceed in that relationship or situation?" Almost invariably everyone said yes. It came while they were still walking faithfully with God. I asked why they didn't heed the warning, and virtually all of them said they rationalized it away.

6. *Many described their sudden behavioral patterns as totally uncharacteristic.* Most mentioned that family, close friends, and associates also noticed uncharacteristic behavior. Anyone who confronted them, however, faced their defensiveness and rationalizations.

7. *Virtually all of them described feelings and practices of isolation.* Satan loves isolation. He wants to draw the believer out of healthy relationships into isolated relationships and out of healthy practices into secretive, unhealthy practices. He purposely woos us away from those who might openly recognize the seduction and call his hand on it. Let's beware of anything that separates us from godly people.

8. *Deception and some level of secrecy were involved.* Satan loves secrets. He wants things to stay in the dark because he knows the moment we expose it to the light of God, he's finished.

The nature of seductive deception is that the lies are often well masked for a while. We are undoubtedly caught in a stronghold of deception when we're starting to "have to lie" to explain our behavior. We reason that others wouldn't understand, but the real reason is that the deceived soon deceive.

Do you relate to any of the eight common claims we have studied today? ❑ Yes ❑ No If so, which ones?

____

____

Common Claims of the Seduced, Part 2

"Be self-controlled and alert. Your enemy the devil prowls around like a roaring lion looking for someone to devour" (1 Pet. 5:8).

Today we will examine eight more common claims of the seduced. Remember, this list is given to help you discern whether you are being or have been seduced.

9. *Many described overwhelming feelings of powerlessness.* Believers are only powerless in their own strength, and God has promised to provide a way of escape for every temptation.

If you've never been hit by a satanic tidal wave, you're inclined to think that walking away from any sin is a matter of making a simple decision. You may never have experienced the feeling of being completely overpowered. Satan's attempt is to inspire a feeling so strong that it eclipses the truth.

The next common denominator could be one major reason why seduction is not easy to walk away from.

10. *Many described something we'll call an addictive nature to the seductive sin.* They can't fully explain some of the things they felt in the heat of the battle any more than I can explain how I felt in times of my severest warfare. I'm not saying anyone fully understands it. I just asked them to try to describe it. I'm bringing to the table what completely independent sources told—and they didn't know anyone else had said something similar.

How do you think a person could develop an addiction to seductive sin? ________________________________

11. *Most utterly hated what they were doing.* Almost every person I interviewed testified that they hated their ungodly behavior but for a season were drawn to it like a magnet. Part of Satan's ploy is to make his victims feel addicted and powerless.

Sometimes people can describe a time of rebellion with a mischievous grin and even admit to having enjoyed it, but I have never heard a godly person who was seduced by the enemy say he could look back on the time with a smile. All will tell you it filled their lives with shame, and they ended up being sickened by it.

12. *The seduction lasted only for a season.* The time frames vary, but people with a genuine heart for God cannot remain in a practice of sin. At some point they will cry out in total desperation for deliverance. For those who have walked closely with God, the desire for a return to His intimate favor finally exceeds the lure of their seducer. In the end, Satan cannot cut it because he can't sustain it. Those who know the truth will finally recognize the lie.

Satan cannot possessively lay hold of us, keep us in a grip, or touch us in a way that will utterly destroy us. We may feel destroyed, but we are not. Christ preserves us from Satan's ultimate intent—our total destruction.

13. *Many describe a period of a spiritual numbness of sorts.* They often report not feeling the expected feelings of immediate devastation. Many reported that "it just didn't seem real for a while." I'm not sure how Satan

does it, but I think he does everything he can to suspend godly sorrow. Godly sorrow brings repentance (2 Cor. 7:10); he wants to delay repentance as long as possible.

The victim has also resisted the warnings of the Holy Spirit and finally quenched Him enough that the normal spiritual feelings are temporarily diluted. To anyone who has ever truly loved God, those feelings do come. And when they finally come, the sorrow is almost unbearable.

14. *Many used the same peculiar word to describe what they had experienced.* Over and over I have heard the word *web* coming from those trying to find a word to describe what they felt they had escaped.

15. *Many describe the aftermath as a time of slowly increasing awareness rather than an instant wake-up.* Many people describe the season following their separation from the seducer like coming out from under the influence of a drug. Coming out from under the influence of this very powerful thing they couldn't define was like slowly getting a drug out of their system.

The simplicity of Christ means we adhere to one ultimate influence. When our minds are opened to the powerful, virtually hypnotic influence of the Devil, we are as unstable as a staggering drunk. Just as it requires time for other kinds of toxins to be washed out of our systems, it takes time for the poison the Evil One has poured into our minds to drain.

16. *Feelings of devastation and indescribable sorrow finally came, ushering in deep repentance.* Nominal or halfhearted Christians may come out of a season of defeat without excessive sorrow, but those who were wholeheartedly, sincerely, and purely devoted to Christ finally experience such a devastation that they often feel they can't go on.

Review the 16 claims we studied the last two days. Place a check (✓) by the ones you are struggling with now or have struggled with in the past. If you are not dealing with some of these issues personally, perhaps you know people who are. Write their initials in the margin and intercede on their behalf.

Next week we will see how a godly person could be vulnerable to the kind of mess we just described.

NOTES

To the Leader:

This study has great potential to alter the course of people's lives. Approach your role as a Bible study leader with much prayer, preparation, and dependence on the Holy Spirit's wisdom and guidance.

Before the Session

Be prepared to read 1 John 5:18 from *The Amplified Bible* for step 6 (see *www.biblegateway.com*).

During the Session

1. Ask if learners think Satan is on a massive campaign to seduce the saints. Ask for examples to back up their answers. Explore why they think Satan has become even more active in attacking Christians. OR Ask participants to name some of the bloodiest battles in history. [Samples: Gettysburg, Shiloh, D-Day, Verdun, Stalingrad] Inquire: *Where do you think the most brutal battles take place today?* Explain that vicious battles occur daily in the lives of believers as Satan seeks to destroy them. FOR EITHER OPTION Use the introduction on page 91 to state the goals and three-part format of this study. Share: *Some of us may see this title* When Godly People Do Ungodly Things *and think we don't need this study. Why do we need to be concerned if we think we don't need to be concerned about being seduced by Satan?* Ask someone to read 1 Corinthians 10:12.
2. Request a volunteer to read 2 Corinthians 11:3. Ask: *What did Paul fear for the Corinthian Christians?* Describe the believers for whom he was concerned. Discuss the first activity in Day 1 (p. 92). Point out that the only one not shocked by the seduction of Christians is God. He told us this was coming. Discuss the activities related to 2 Thessalonians 2 and Matthew 24 in Day 1. Direct participants to read Revelation 12:12 in their Bibles and state how Satan feels about his time drawing to an end. Ask: *According to 1 Peter 5:8, what is Satan trying to do in the time he has left?*
3. Ask: *Why is knowing your enemy essential to winning the war? How is our enemy described in John 12:31 and 16:11* (p. 94)*?* Ask what two clues let us know there is a greater ruler than this prince. [He'll be cast out; he has been judged.] Discuss how Satan is like a lame duck politician. Ask: *How might a wicked president abuse his power in the time he has left in office?* Discuss how that somewhat describes what Christians are

NOTES

enduring at the hands of Satan during this age. Invite volunteers to share what insights they have gained into who Satan is. Discuss: *How do these insights frighten, comfort, challenge, and/or encourage you?*

4. Ask why sexual seduction is one of Satan's most powerful weapons against believers. Discuss the first activity of Day 3 (p. 97). Discuss avenues Satan has of sexually seducing believers that he didn't have 50 years ago. Discuss the ramifications of pornography. Invite someone to read 1 Timothy 4:1. Ask what Satan desires for each of our lives. Explore why sexual perversion may make some Christians feel they have to turn away from the faith. This study is written to urge fallen believers to not turn away but to turn back to God.
5. Guide a discussion of the 16 common claims of the seduced using these questions: *Give examples of how temptations can catch a Christian off guard. Why are we vulnerable at spiritually high times? How can obsessing over someone or something lead to a devastating fall? What are some red flags that might indicate we're headed in a dangerous direction? How does Hebrews 10:24-25 tell us we can prevent isolation that can lead to falling? How can the promise of 1 Corinthians 10:13 help you overcome feelings of powerlessness? What are some seductive sins to which Christians become addicted and how do they develop those addictions? How do you think Satan numbs Christians and why does he want to prevent us from having godly sorrow? Why do you think many godly people who did ungodly things used the term* web *to describe their experiences?*
6. Read 1 John 5:18 from The Amplified Bible. Ask how that verse supports the truth that the seduction will only last for a season. Ask: *Why can Satan attack us but not get a full grip on us?* Explain that Satan can bruise us and beat us, but he can never penetrate our spiritual skin to destroy our souls. The value of knowing these claims shared by so many who have been seduced is that perhaps they can prevent other Christians from the devastation of being battered by Satan.
7. Close in prayer, using the prayer at the conclusion of Day 3 (p. 98).

God's Permissive Will

day One

Susceptible to Seduction

This week we will consider how a devoted servant of Jesus Christ could become vulnerable to such powerfully demonic seduction. The people we're talking about were not living under the dominion of any sin when they were attacked. Sin is not where the enemy most often gets his foothold on the godly. Rather, the enemy more often latches on to weakness—or maybe I should say a hidden spot of vulnerability. Satan knows weakness can turn to sin in a heartbeat when exposed to the right amount of pressure.

"This is my prayer: that your love may abound more and more in knowledge and depth of insight, so that you may be able to discern what is best and may be pure and blameless until the day of Christ" (Phil. 1:9-10).

I have become more and more convinced that victims of seduction share certain vulnerabilities at the time of their attack. If you have never been seduced but share these vulnerabilities, child of God, be warned! You could be headed for the nightmare of your life!

1. *Ignorance.* The number one element that sets believers up for seduction is ignorance! I tried to think of a prettier word, but this is the one the Bible uses. What we do not know can hurt us!

Throughout the remainder of the list, you will see signs of ignorance—things the seduced did not know. One of the most common forms of ignorance was that none of them knew this kind of thing could happen.

2. *Spiritual passion that exceeds biblical knowledge.* Read 2 Corinthians 11:3 (printed in margin). The person described has wholehearted devotion to Christ, but the mind is still vulnerable. Most of ours are too—until we have a horrible scare that teaches us to love God with our whole mind and not just our whole heart.

"I am fearful, lest that even as the serpent beguiled Eve by his cunning, so your minds may be corrupted and seduced from wholehearted and sincere and pure devotion to Christ" (2 Cor. 11:3, AMP).

If we don't have the knowledge of God, we are ill equipped to recognize imaginations that exalt themselves over God. We can't just have knowledge about warfare to defeat Satan. Our only means of getting it is through an intense relationship with God through His Word.

Many of those in ministry who fell for seduction had gotten so busy doing the work of God they slipped away from pure intimacy with God.

Allow me to offer a word of caution on the other side of this double-edged issue. A head full of biblical knowledge without a heart passionately in love with Christ is terribly dangerous—a stronghold waiting to happen. Satan knows that we all long for passion. If we are not given to godly passion, we will be tempted by counterfeits.

3. *A lack of discernment.* Discernment means to see or understand the difference. Discernment will be one of the most important criteria in the devoted believer's life to provide protection from seduction.

What does each of the following verses have to say about discernment?
Proverbs 14:33 ______________________________
Proverbs 19:25 ______________________________
Proverbs 28:11 ______________________________
Philippians 1:9-10 ____________________________

Discernment is critical. Do you see how susceptible any of us can be to seduction without it? Celebrate the fact that God honors the heartfelt petition for discernment and will graciously give it and more.

4. *A lack of self-discernment.* This one is so important! We commit some sins willfully and presumptuously. We commit others inadvertently. The former flows from rebellion and the latter from error, ignorance, and weakness. It's all sin, but rebellion is not the only way to get into trouble. Our weaknesses and areas of ignorance are huge vulnerabilities to seduction, which can quickly lead to sins committed inadvertently.

We know that Satan's seduction is purposeful, scheming, and utterly intended for evil. It is well planned and timed; nothing about it is accidental or coincidental. In such cases, are the mortals he chooses to use as the agents of seduction always evil, malicious, and completely intentional?

According to Scripture, Satan uses several types of humans in his seductive schemes. We find one type in 1 Timothy 4:1-2.

What does Paul say some will do (1 Tim. 4:1)?

____

What happens to those who follow deceiving spirits (v. 2)?

____

Paul presented a pretty scathing indictment against those who are such willing servants of Satan's seductions!

We are vastly helped when we recognize our own errors, our own transgressions, and the ways in which we've committed sins inadvertently. We are so quick to acknowledge the errors of others, but one of our best defenses is to recognize where we've gone wrong and where our personal weak places are.

Trusting God with Our Past

Today we need to deal with weaknesses caused by exposure to or experience with false worship or depravity in the past.

Paul was worried about the Corinthian church because they had been exposed to so much false worship and depravity. Many of them had come directly from those practices. They had fallen for such false teaching in the past that he feared they could be had again: "You put up with it easily enough" (2 Cor. 11:4). Not only that, but they were still surrounded by ungodliness in their attempts to live godly lives.

Corinth was vile even by our standards today. Not unlike us, they were constantly exposed to the worship of false idols, sexual looseness, and nudity. Their exposure was literal; ours is often through billboards, magazine covers, television shows, and, perhaps even worse, commercials!

Any level of exposure can open a door in the mind that Satan might one day use for his advantage. Some of us were exposed to things we should never have seen as children. For instance, being exposed to pornography can take a profound toll on the later life, and Satan often makes sure it does.

Experience can open an even wider door than exposure. Satan would be foolish not to try to exploit our past experiences. How many people have come to salvation in Jesus Christ and been forgiven and made new only for Satan to continue to taunt, accuse, remind, and tempt them with past memories of sinful activities? God keeps no record of believers' wrongs, but you can be sure Satan does.

We have such unbelief concerning our new identities in Christ that we practically let Satan get away with murder—the murder of a new self-concept defined in the Word of God.

Either as a child or an adult, what events or experiences do you have in your past that Satan has or might use to seduce you? Check all that apply.

- ❑ **Abuse when I was a child**
- ❑ **Parents who did not know how to show love**
- ❑ **Death of parent(s)**
- ❑ **Divorce in home**
- ❑ **Rape as a child or adult**
- ❑ **Marriage to an abusive spouse**
- ❑ **Addiction to some drug or behavior**
- ❑ **Performance based self-worth**
- ❑ **Other** ______________________________

Do some journaling in the margin about how these elements have (1) created vulnerabilities in your life and (2) created additional opportunities for you to minister to others.

Dear one, if we don't let God deal with every part of our pasts, our hurts, our secrets, our errors in judgment, our mistakes, our sins, or the handicaps in our backgrounds, any one of them can be like a hibernating bear.

Satan plays hardball. When we have a disaster, we can count on his being right there confronting us at our weakest, most vulnerable point.

"We can't just put our pasts behind us. We've got to put our pasts in front of God."—Beth Moore

Would Satan take advantage of a helpless child? Yes! Would he descend on the life of a grieving mother? Without question! Would he capitalize on a past we've tried so hard to put behind us? Count on it! We can't just put our pasts behind us. We've got to put our pasts in front of God. Satan is inconceivably mean and will take advantage of any unfinished business.

We can do something about our pasts. We can take them to Jesus! We need Him to take full authority over them so they are no longer a playground for the enemy. He longs to reframe our pasts and let us see them against the backdrop of His glory.

God never abuses His authority. He also never shames. Do you remember the woman at the well? After her encounter with Jesus, she ran into town telling about her experience.

She wasn't ashamed! Do you know why? Because when Christ takes authority over our pasts and we allow Him to confront them, treat them, and heal them, we exchange our shame for dignity!

My past sins aren't invitations to Satan anymore, and yours don't have to be either. God is so inconceivably faithful. Trust Him with every inch of your past, present, and future! Until you do, you are susceptible to seduction.

Is any area in your life still a weakness? Perhaps you have already confessed it and asked God to forgive you, but you have never asked God to heal you completely, redeem your past, restore your life, sanctify you entirely, and help you forgive your past. Would you be willing to do that now? If so, write a prayer in the margin expressing the desire of your heart.

Being Aware of Satan's Schemes

Why in the world would God allow someone with wholehearted, sincere, pure devotion to Christ to get caught in the snare of demonic seduction? God develops strength in His children through various trials and tribulations, but demonic seduction? What purpose could it possibly serve? It doesn't even seem fair, does it?

"Put on the full armor of God so that you can take your stand against the devil's schemes" (Eph. 6:11).

The difference between our everyday temptations and a pointed, intentionally destructive demonic seduction is the difference between a snowball and an avalanche. We can see the added intensification in varying seasons of attack even in the earthly life of Christ. He no doubt had temptations on an ongoing basis but perhaps nothing compared to the full-scale season of temptation in the wilderness.

In the following example, circle clues that suggest this man was being seduced.

I heard a testimony about a pastor in his early 60s who had walked with God all his believing life. Although he had amazing compassion for a man who had never really experienced failure, he had no reference point for understanding how Christian people could get into some of the messes he had counseled. He was a godly man and was neither boastful of his good track record nor judgmental of others who were slightly muddier. In his heart and mind, he simply did not understand.

When this pastor reached his late 50s, something totally unexpected happened. A season of darkness fell upon him: an indescribable heaviness of spirit that neither he nor others could tie to anything circumstantial or physiological. As if the darkness and depression were not enough to cope with, he then began to struggle with lustful, truly pornographic thoughts unlike anything he had ever experienced. He was literally bombarded with evil thoughts.

"Be strong in the Lord [be empowered through your union with Him]; draw your strength from Him [that strength which His boundless might provides]. Put on God's whole armor [the armor of a heavy-armed soldier which God supplies], that you may be able successfully to stand up against [all] the strategies and the deceits of the devil. For we are not wrestling with flesh and blood [contending only with physical opponents], but against the despotisms, against the powers, against [the master spirits who are] the world rulers of this present darkness, against the spirit forces of wickedness in the heavenly (supernatural) sphere. Therefore put on God's complete armor, that you may be able to resist and stand your ground on the evil day [of danger], and having done all [the crisis demands], to stand [firmly in your place]" (Eph. 6:10-13, AMP).

He endured the months of suffering and temptation without physically committing adultery, but he did temporarily succumb to uncharacteristic behavior, and those around him were not unaffected. As the season ended, he was personally devastated and found himself asking the question so many others have asked: "What was that?" That was seduction.

Those who aren't among the high-risk believers are still not immune to temptation. No doubt, this man's low-risk profile guarded him against more grievous trespasses in his season of temptation, but it did not keep him from being bombarded.

Our question, however, is why would God allow a man of his character to be assaulted by the Evil One in the manner he was? Although Ephesians 6 does not tell us why, it certainly alerts us to the reality of a dangerous enemy and a furious war.

Read Ephesians 6:10-13 printed in the margin. Underline the phrases that speak most to you.

What admonition does Paul give in these verses?

____

Why are we to put on the armor of God?

____

The Devil does not work haphazardly but carefully, methodically, weaving and spinning, and watching for just the right time. He draws out plans and executes them very carefully. He sets traps for the express purpose of wreaking destruction in the lives of the saints.

Earlier we discussed that anything God does, Satan attempts to counterfeit. One of the first biblical principles most believers learn concerning their new agenda is that God has a plan for their lives. Please hear this with your whole heart, believer: so does Satan.

Often our times of assault will come when we're least expecting them. But why does God allow them at all? Since God's ways are higher than ours and His thoughts far beyond us, we won't wholly be able to answer this question. We simply do not have the tools to understand God. We can, however, discover some answers that are available to us.

If you have ever been seduced, think back to the way your seduction unfolded. List the method Satan used to get to you.

____

God never appoints us to sin. Even when He tests His children, His purpose is to prove godly character … or perhaps to show us the lack thereof. God never tempts us to sin, nor does He ever fail to provide a way of escape. In our next lesson we are going to see scriptural evidence exists that Satan has to gain permission to wage war against a believer in Christ.

As you end today's study, ask God for spiritual discernment that you will be aware of Satan's schemes.

The Testing of Job

"The LORD said to Satan, 'Very well, then, everything he has is in your hands, but on the man himself do not lay a finger' " (Job 1:12).

Both Old and New Testament Scripture support the idea that Satan has to gain God's permission to wage war upon one of His redeemed. Job 1 is a perfect example. Many scholars believe the Book of Job is one of the oldest books of the Bible. I find that very significant since it concerns a man, His God, and an unseen war.

Read Job 1:1-22. Do you realize Job endured the entire excruciating ordeal without ever knowing he was in the middle of a match between the God of the universe and the head dragon of hell? Even at the conclusion of the Old Testament book, Job still had no idea. He had learned plenty about the sovereignty of God, but he still had no concept of the faith God had shown in him. Don't you think Job would have had an easier time if God had said, "Listen, son. I know this is horribly painful, but something much bigger than you know is at stake here. You are a truly righteous man in an unrighteous world. Satan thinks you'll crumble if I draw back some of your protection and blessing. I want him to see that you won't. So, as hard as this is, you stand firm! "

How would you feel in a time of testing to hear such a speech from God? ______________________________

That kind of explanation would have made a tremendous difference to me. What could be more motivating than a fierce spirit of competition? If we knew the stakes were high and we were in the middle of a paramount competition, we would throw everything we had into it. The fact is, we are in such a competition. We just don't realize it. Neither did Job. I have wondered over and over what his face looked like when he got to heaven and they told him what was going on in the unseen world while he was down below.

Can you imagine how strangely Job must have felt to realize he had been chosen by God to fight one of the most difficult earthly battles in history? In humanly inexplicable ways, God allowed Job to be tested so harshly because He, God, had faith in him, Job. Amazing.

We're not out of our reach doctrinally to assume that the same huge competition in the heavenlies takes place all around us. That's exactly what Ephesians 6:10-12 says. Who's to say when things really get tough that we, and countless other believers, have not momentarily been chosen to prove faithful to God? If we were in the middle of that kind of competition, wouldn't we want to win? I love knowing God's team is always going to win, but I want to be part of the victory myself.

When Satan turns up the heat, I often say something like this to myself: *You have no idea what's going on. This could be really important. Stand firm and don't give the yell leaders of hell anything to cheer about. God is for you.*

The battle is rough and sometimes seems unbearable, but God is always for us. Why does He let our opponents hit us so hard? To prove that we, mortal flesh and blood and self-centered by nature, really are for God.

Perhaps you're thinking, *But I've already blown my play. I failed my test.* Do you want to talk about someone who has blown some plays? I have! But God didn't take me off the team. He took me to the locker room, gave me a little chewing out, a lot of coaching, a little cheering, and sent me back onto the field. I have made most of my plays since then. Sometimes they're awkward, late, and not very pretty, but the points still count.

What encourages you most about the ideas we've been discussing?

____

Are you still living? Then there's still time on the clock. Are you still a Christian? Then you haven't been taken off the team. Get up and fight! God wants to prove to the kingdom of hell that you will get up and you will prove faithful to God. Those who have been wholeheartedly, sincerely, and purely devoted to Christ, no matter how they've been knocked down, will not stay under that pile of opposing players. They will call upon the power of their God and get up. And the players of hell will go flying.

What about you? Have you been called on to make a play and blown it? If so, confess it to God right now and accept His forgiveness. Now get up and get back into the game ... the clock is ticking. Win one for the King!

The Sifting of Peter

When I'm writing a Bible study, I spend more time back in the world of Scripture than I do out in my own. I have a feeling God thinks I'm safer if I stay inside. Some of these Bible figures have become like good buddies. Peter's one of them. He's given me a lot of hope through the years. He spent a lot of his time with Christ big on passion and small on smarts. Been there.

Read Matthew 16:15-19. No matter what our differing doctrinal stands may be, that's big by any standard. God builds the church on Jesus Christ (1 Cor. 3:11) and the testimony the disciples would preach concerning Him (Matt. 28:19), but no doubt Christ was going to make Peter a major player.

" 'Simon, Simon, Satan has asked to sift you as wheat. But I have prayed for you, Simon, that your faith may not fail. And when you have turned back, strengthen your brothers.' " But he replied, 'Lord, I am ready to go with you to prison and to death.' Jesus answered, 'I tell you, Peter, before the rooster crows today, you will deny three times that you know me' " (Luke 22:31-34).

Fast forward to the time when the things Christ prophesied began to be fulfilled at the Passover meal, and Jesus told them that one among them would betray Him.

In the verses in the margin, underline Satan's request and circle Jesus' prayer for Peter.

Read Luke 22:56-62. Within only a few hours, what had Peter done? ________________________________

The implications of this account are huge to a follower of Jesus Christ. I believe that Satan had to obtain permission to move outside his usual perimeters and launch a full-scale attack on one of God's children. Satan can and does seek permission to launch excessive attacks on the children of God. God can and sometimes does grant Satan permission to launch such attacks.

I'd like to suggest that Peter's encounter with the Evil One wasn't just a test. Peter's test was a sift. Only one reason exists why God would give Satan permission to sift a dearly loved, devoted disciple: because something needs sifting. God's answer to Satan's petition to sift Peter as wheat would have been denied had Peter not contained something that needed sifting.

Had Christ made a mistake in choosing Peter? Was He sorry? Hardly. He'd made no mistake. Christ told Peter that he would be a powerhouse, and He meant it. Christ also knew that Peter had no means whatsoever of becoming the person He had called him to be. Like all of us, Peter was far too weak in his natural self (see Rom. 6:19).

Read 1 Thessalonians 5:23-24. Write verse 24 in the margin.

Christ called Peter knowing every flaw in him. He gave that flawed apostle a new assignment and a new name. By heaven, the call would be accomplished even if Christ had to do it Himself. I believe Jesus loved Peter's passion, but His cherished disciple also had some ingredients that could prove less palatable to the call. Everything standing between Simon the fisherman and Peter the rock needed to go.

Satan had a sieve. Christ had a purpose. The two collided. Satan got used. Peter got sifted. For reasons only our wise, trustworthy God knows, the most effective and long-lasting way He could get the Simon out of Peter was a sifting by Satan. He was right. You see, the One who called us is faithful, and He will do whatever it takes to sanctify us to fulfill our callings. Yes, it's that important. Remember, huge things are going on out there that we just don't understand.

I believe God allows Satan a certain amount of leash where believers are concerned, but I am convinced that if he wants more than his daily allowance, he has to get permission. None of us is less important to Christ than Peter, John, or the Apostle Paul. He would never take lightly one of Satan's attacks on His followers. For Satan to launch a full-scale attack of seduction on a wholehearted, sincere, and purely devoted follower of Christ, I believe he has to get permission.

Beloved, are you being sifted? Has God permitted the enemy to launch a full-scale attack against you? God knows what He's doing. He isn't looking the other way, and He's not being mean to you. Maybe this is the only way He can get you to attend to the old so He can do something new. Grab onto Him for dear life!

Have you ever experienced a time of sifting?
❑ Yes ❑ No If so, describe it in the margin.

NOTES

To the Leader:

You will have class members who have experienced some of the devastating attacks you will discuss throughout this study, and they may approach you for counsel. Unless you are a trained counselor, put them in contact with a member of your church staff, especially if they are of the opposite sex. This is serious, and you need to watch yourself carefully.

Before the Session

Obtain index cards to use in step 4.

During the Session

1. Ask: *Were there bullies in your school? What kinds of kids did these bullies pick on?* OR Ask participants if they enjoy wild animal shows. Ask: *In the animal kingdom, what kind of prey do predators most prefer to attack?* FOR EITHER OPTION Read Psalm 10:2 (in NIV if possible). Declare that Satan is a bully and a predator who preys on the weak. Our weaknesses make us vulnerable targets for demonic seduction.
2. Ask: *Is it true that "What you don't know can't hurt you"? Why?* Invite someone to read Hebrews 5:2. Explore the relationship between ignorance, weakness, and going astray.
3. Examine why spiritual passion and biblical knowledge must be balanced to avoid becoming a vulnerable target. Discuss the first activity of Day 1 (p. 106). Ask: *Why are Christians susceptible targets if they lack discernment?* Discuss the difference between discernment and self-discernment. Request that the class share examples of willful and inadvertent sins. Ask: *How can sinning without even realizing you are rebelling make you susceptible to seduction?*
4. Explain that exposure to depravity is another area that causes weakness in believers. Ask how Christians today are exposed to depravity and how that makes us susceptible to seduction. Determine how the past experiences listed in Day 2 (p. 108) can make a Christian a vulnerable target for Satan's attacks. Discuss: *Why is putting our past behind us a dangerous thing to do? How can we put our experiences in front of Jesus instead? How can that protect us from seduction?* Distribute an index card to each participant. Ask them to prayerfully and confidentially write down what their personal weak places are. Encourage them to later review the common claims of the seduced from Week 1 and check for signs they are being seduced in those vulnerable areas.

NOTES

5. Emphasize that we must be aware we are at war with a ruthless enemy who will attack at our weakest point. Ask someone to read Ephesians 6:10-13 (p. 110). Explore that passage with questions such as: *What is the only remedy for our weaknesses? What are we wrestling with? Why is that so much harder than fighting physical opponents? What does Paul tell us to do and why?* Ask why Satan schemes and strategizes against believers. Explain that Jeremiah 29:11 declares God's purpose for our lives. Challenge learners to read that verse in their Bible and reword it negatively to state Satan's plan for each person.
6. Share: *We know we are under attack by Satan but what we really want to know is why God allows those assaults at all. We will never fully understand why but we can be assured that Satan must seek God's permission before he can attack a believer.* Organize the class into three groups. Ask Group 1 to describe Job from Job 1:1-5. Ask Group 2 to describe the interchange between God and Satan in Job 1:6-12. Ask Group 3 to describe what happened to Job in Job 1:13-19. After a few moments, allow groups to share. Ask: *If you had been Job, would it have helped to know you were involved in a battle bigger than yourself? Why? How would it help you fight seduction if you knew God believed in your faithfulness enough that He allowed it to be tested? What will God do if you fail your test? What should we do when/if we fail our tests?*
7. Ask a volunteer to read Luke 22:31-34. Discuss the first activity of Day 5 (p. 114). Lead the class to discuss what Job and Peter had in common. [They were sincerely devoted to God. Satan had to ask permission to attack them. God, in His Sovereignty, allowed it.] Ask why God allowed Peter's sifting. Ask for two volunteers to read Job 23:10 and 1 Peter 1:6-7. Talk about what these two men concluded was the purpose of testing, even if it was through a difficult time of demonic attack. Point out that both men came out stronger on the other side.
8. Ask participants to draw on what they've learned in this study to give reasons why God would allow someone with a wholehearted, sincere, pure devotion to Christ to get caught in the snare of demonic seduction. Ask: *Where's the hope in this lesson for you?* Close in prayer.

The Watchman

Seduce-Proofing Our Lives

This week we will learn how to seduce-proof our lives. First Thessalonians 5:23-24 holds the key that locks the gate where seduction creeps in. Even if our ships get off course and we find ourselves in an ocean of vulnerability, this passage will guide us back to safe harbor.

"May God himself, the God of peace, sanctify you through and through. May your whole spirit, soul and body be kept blameless at the coming of our Lord Jesus Christ. The one who calls you is faithful and he will do it" (1 Thess. 5:23-24).

What do you think it means to be sanctified through and through? ______________________________

In 1 Thessalonians 5:16-25 we find one of the most concentrated segments of Scripture in the entire New Testament that describes exactly what you and I are looking for: a seduce-proofed believer.

Read 1 Thessalonians 5:16-25 in your Bible. List in the margin words or phrases that describe ways to become a seduce-proofed believer.

A Concise Profile of a Seduce-Proofed Christian

This powerful Scripture provides a picture of what a seduce-proofed life looks like. Let's consider each element of this description.

1. *He is happy in his faith.* "Rejoice always!" (v. 16, HCSB). The Apostle Paul seemed to be saying, "For heaven's sake, be happy in your faith! That's one reason you have it!"

Too many of us somehow believe that we lack maturity if we wish that the Christian life weren't just good for us like a bowl of bran but that it could also occasionally make us happy like a chocolate malt!

Guess what? You have complete biblical permission to be happy in your faith and to be bold enough to ask why if you're not!

2. *She abstains from evil.* "Stay away from every form of evil" (v. 22, HCSB). God gives us the power to abstain from evil by being happy in our faith. Certainly many other things can add happiness to our lives, but they are detoxified and made safe to believers when their primary source of happiness is faith in Jesus. Without happiness in Christ, any other source of joy can become a tool for seduction. Nothing will make you consistently happier than a vibrant relationship with Jesus Christ.

3. *He is unceasing in prayer.* "Pray without ceasing" (v. 17, KJV). Paul was talking about a perpetual line of open communication with God throughout the day. We're not given to this kind of mentality naturally, so we have to learn how to pray unceasingly. This will be an ongoing pursuit and one we aren't likely to master, but isn't prayer just that? A pursuit?

A pray-without-ceasing relationship means seeing everything against the backdrop of God's presence. Even listening to a powerful worship CD while putting dishes in the dishwasher can be prayer without ceasing. Constant communication. Sometimes saying a lot, sometimes saying a little, but living every moment as if He were right there. After all, He is, isn't He?

How do you feel about the concept of praying unceasingly?

- ❑ **It bores me.**
- ❑ **It excites me.**
- ❑ **It makes me nervous.**
- ❑ **I wonder if I can do it.**
- ❑ **It's for the spiritually mature.**
- ❑ **I want to begin now!**

What does unceasing communication have to do with protecting ourselves from the enemy? How often do loneliness and insecurity open a soul to seduction? Our next exhortation helps combat that.

4. *She is thankful and gives thanks.* "Give thanks in everything" (v. 18, HCSB). Seduce-proofed people live in active gratitude. Dissatisfaction is a stronghold waiting to happen. An unsatisfied soul should never be ignored. Ongoing or chronic feelings of dissatisfaction are red flags that need to be inspected. Such feelings may mean something vital is missing, and we need to seek God without delay.

Other times, nagging dissatisfaction can be little more than the byproduct of living in an overindulged society. Many times we don't have a knowledge problem; we have an obedience problem. Be thankful and actively give thanks.

List in the margin things for which you are thankful.

5. *He doesn't quench the Spirit.* "Don't stifle the Spirit" (v. 19, HCSB). Nothing will be more important to us in seduce-proofing our lives than practicing the Holy Spirit-filled or controlled life. Without the full empowerment of the Holy Spirit, we have no defense against the enemy's schemes.

God created us for the fire of the Holy Spirit! If we quench His fire, we'll look for another one elsewhere. That's when we're liable to get burned.

Think back for a moment to a scene captured in Exodus 3. Moses heard the voice of God coming from a burning bush. The fire itself was not what made Moses want to take a second look. A fire wasn't unusual. The fire was unusual because the flames were not burning up the bush. God's is the only fire that can consume an object without eventually destroying it. Anger destroys. Rage destroys. Lust destroys. No other fiery passion in our souls will ever guard us from getting burned.

Seduce-Proofing, Part 2

Today we will continue to discover ways to seduce-proof our lives using 1 Thessalonians 5:16-25. Take a moment to read the passage again and refresh your memory.

"Who can discern his errors? Forgive my hidden faults. Keep your servant also from willful sins; may they not rule over me. Then will I be blameless, innocent of great transgression" (Ps. 19:12-13).

6. *She does not despise instruction, exhortation, or warning.* "Don't despise prophecies" (v. 20, HCSB). Not only is the seduce-proofed individual a hearer and doer of the Word, she also does not despise the instructions, exhortations, or warnings of those sent by God.

Keep in mind that these instructions, exhortations, or warnings may not come face-to-face. They may come from a sermon, a Christian radio broadcast, or a Christian book that God has purposely placed in our hands. They may also come from a source less agreeable to our palates.

Not only do I like to pick out the advice I want; but I also I like to pick out who gives it to me! God doesn't always send our favorite messengers with His well-pointed exhortations. We have to learn to listen anyway.

Seek godly counsel. If the counsel of the wise seems to match the sense you get from the Holy Spirit after much prayer, go with their advice no matter how badly your flesh wants to do otherwise!

7. *He tests and proves all things until he recognizes what is good.* "Test all things. Hold on to what is good" (v. 21, HCSB). If we'll learn to test and prove all things, we'll also come to agreement with God-sent exhortation or warning. I can't think of many characteristics more vital in the profile of the seduce-proofed person.

Good and evil do not always appear black and white in our technicolor world. Furthermore, a huge chasm can separate goodwill from God's will. I'm slowly learning to test and prove all things until I can recognize what is good. I still find the wait excruciating at times.

8. *She allows God to sanctify her through and through.* "May God himself, the God of peace, sanctify you through and through" (v. 23). Our safety, joy, fulfillment, and wholeness are all found in allowing God to completely invade us through and through. Nothing withheld. Nothing off-limits.

I don't mean perfected. I just mean surrendered and under the safekeeping of God's dominion. Anything of our experiences, issues, or weaknesses that we don't deliberately set apart to the safekeeping of Christ's dominion sits like a wide-open target under the nose of the lion.

Can you think of any area of your life you are withholding from God? Be honest with yourself; God already knows. Write it in the margin.

9. *His whole spirit, soul, and body are kept blameless.* "May your spirit, soul, and body be kept sound and blameless" (v. 23, HCSB). Perfection in this lifetime is not going to happen. Christ's primary guard against seduction was that He was totally fulfilled by His Father's love, presence, and will. Developing perfection is not a reasonable or expected earthly hope for mortals, but I'll tell you what can be the goal: blamelessness!

The psalmists speak often of the coveted condition they describe as "blameless." Read Proverbs 28:18 printed in the margin. What does it tell us about being blameless?

"He whose walk is blameless is kept safe, but he whose ways are perverse will suddenly fall" (Prov. 28:18).

"He whose walk is blameless is kept ______________."

How can we be safe from seduction? By developing a blameless walk.

Read Psalm 19:12-13. What is David's inspired definition of blamelessness?

- ❑ **When we are perfect**
- ❑ **When we are sinless**
- ❑ **When we see Jesus**
- ❑ **When no willful sin is ruling over us**

Living out from under the dominion of willful sin is not only possible, it is our God-given right, our Holy Spirit-empowered reality, and the absolute will of our Father in heaven.

10. *She knows that the One who called her is faithful and He will do it.* "He who calls you is faithful, who also will do it" (v. 24, HCSB). The seduce-proofed woman has no confidence in her flesh. Nor does she dream that either checking off a list of characteristics or performing a catalog of spiritual disciplines has any power to protect her. She knows that God is faithful, and He will do it.

Pause and thank God that He is faithful. God will accomplish His will in your life if you allow Him.

11. *He knows he needs prayer*. "Brothers, pray for us also" (v. 25, HCSB). We need prayer. Especially as the Day is drawing near!

If you can't name several people who actively intercede for you on a consistent basis, get busy enlisting some! Commit to reciprocate, and become an effective intercessor for others. Don't assume that since you've done OK so far without prayer partners that you're not at risk. These are ever-increasing days of wickedness! Start looking. Commanding us to pray for one another is one of the ways God enforces unity in the body of Christ.

"I pray also that the eyes of your heart may be enlightened in order that you may know the hope to which he has called you, the riches of his glorious inheritance in the saints, and his incomparably great power for us who believe. That power is like the working of his mighty strength" (Eph. 1:18 -19).

As we conclude today's lesson, let's practice what Paul just preached to us. Pray for someone who once had wholehearted, sincere, and pure devotion to Christ but who is presently caught in a web of seduction. He or she is in such urgent need. Pray Ephesians 1:18-19 for this brother or sister.

Pray that this "sleeper" would "wake up" and that God would mercifully expose the deeds of darkness and expose the precious life to the light so healing can begin.

Strong Walls

Keith and I need a new fence. The neighbor directly behind us innocently planted a small line of trees right against the fence many years ago. Inch by inch, the roots have grown under our fence and into our yard until the uneven ground has completely unearthed the fence posts. They grew so gradually we didn't notice until the slats were falling, one after the other.

"No temptation has seized you except what is common to man. And God is faithful; he will not let you be tempted beyond what you can bear. But when you are tempted, he will also provide a way out so that you can stand up under it" (1 Cor. 10:13).

Our predicament certainly could be worse. Another person's fence fell down too. Her property was next to a small wildlife park. Both neighbors had quite a lot of acreage, and she raised miniature horses while her neighbor boasted a variety of exotic animals.

How did she realize part of her fence was down? One day she looked up and a male lion was tearing her favorite horse to shreds. True story.

We often don't realize part of our fence is down until Satan is devouring something precious to us right on our own property. He has no right to be on our property, but all he needs is a weak spot in the fence.

What happened to our fence is exactly what happens in our lives when the enemy gains ground that does not belong to him. At some point prior to his complete intrusion, he laid groundwork. This groundwork is often so subtle and seems so harmless that we give it very little notice. Inch by inch, the enemy grows something powerful right on the edge of our fence.

Is the enemy laying groundwork to defeat you?
Do you see areas that need immediate attention?
What are they?

Never assume that just because a smaller problem hasn't exploded into a bigger problem before, it never will. That's exactly what the enemy wants us to think. Don't ever forget what a schemer he is. He loves nothing better than supplying a false sense of security. I pray that God will expose every bit of false security we have!

How does Satan get inside the wall or fence line? He puts pressure on the outside, hoping to get a reaction or some sort of cooperation from the inside. All he needs is one little piece of the fence or wall to crumble, and the lion's in the yard. Satan puts pressure on the wall or fence by raising either temptation or turmoil. One or the other can eventually lead to both.

Satan can put pressure on the fence (or wall) by raising temptation right at the fence line. Remember when we talked about the importance of being happy and satisfied in our faith? If we don't take Christ up on the fullness of joy and satisfaction within our walls, we are still subject to longing glances at life outside our walls.

What about turmoil? One of Satan's most powerful schemes against me came through raising turmoil at my fence line. He knew I was an abuse victim whether or not I had ever faced the fact. He raised all sorts of things at the fence line that quickened emotional reactions in me.

Many of the things he raised at the fence line were nothing but lies, but I was too inexperienced to recognize the deception. Had I allowed God to permeate my life with His sanctifying Holy Spirit and heal me, Satan couldn't have evoked such an inside response from me. I cooperated with the Devil because I had not completely cooperated with God.

Satan did everything he could at that fence line to get a reaction from me on the inside of my temple. Why did God let him? He didn't just let him. He used him. Allowing Satan to call the victim buried within me to the surface became such a teaching tool in the hand of God that I could not ignore it. Nor will I ever forget it.

What are some lessons you had to learn the hard way?

____

Satan hopes to raise such a powerful opposition at the fence line that we lose self-control. In other words, self rejects the control of the Holy Spirit and we give way to things such as anger, bitterness, rage, lust, greed, ambition, and despair.

Whether Satan targets weakness or sin makes little difference to him if he can cause us to temporarily reject the authority and sanctifying power of the Holy Spirit. If he can accomplish his goal, just one little area of the wall tumbles down.

God reserves the right to say what gets to enter the gates and what does not. When we establish sturdy walls, we don't have to live in fear. We just let the walls do their jobs. Don't ever forget that Satan can't get in from the outside without an invitation from the inside.

Secret Places

Read Ezekiel 8:1-10,12 and meditate on every word. What did Ezekiel see through the hole in the wall?

____

Ezekiel 8:7 tells us the Spirit took Ezekiel to the entrance of the court. The inner court could represent what is private to us without necessarily being sacred. In other words, the secret places. The most secret chamber of our personal lives that we might consider outside the sacred could be the mind. Many of us may not be committing grievous sins with our bodies, but we are entertaining them in the recesses of our minds.

When David the psalmist spoke about the inner parts (see Ps. 51:6), he referred to the secret places of the mind and heart (or emotions). After his headlong dive into a pit of sin, he realized how much he needed "truth in the inner parts" and "wisdom in the inmost place." We kid ourselves into thinking that sin is safe in the secret places.

"Whatever is true, whatever is noble, whatever is right, whatever is pure, whatever is lovely, whatever is admirable—if anything is excellent or praiseworthy—think about such things" (Phil. 4:8).

The mind is often the last inner chamber we allow God to sanctify. One reason is because it is a never-ending challenge to keep clean, and we sometimes adopt the attitude, "Why bother?" But we must bother because the mind is the biggest battlefield we have on which our spiritual battles are fought. Even our feelings eventually bow down to our thoughts.

If we change the way we think, before long our thoughts change the way we feel. All sin begins in the mind, and untold secret sin is allowed to flourish there. But not without effect. Sooner or later.

We can't be perfect or sinless, nor can we find some legalistic means of controlling every thought we have. But God can clean up our negative or impure minds! If we don't let Him, our minds will taint our hearts and ultimately affect our actions. Remember how the Apostle Paul said the serpent could get to those with wholehearted, sincere, and pure devotion to Christ? By seducing and corrupting their minds (see 2 Cor. 11:2-3)!

What are we doing behind the hole in the wall? in the secret places of the mind? What are our idols right there in the inner chambers—those no one else knows about? Is there a mess behind that hole in the wall?

You cannot diminish God's love with impure or negative thoughts, but you can diminish your awareness and enjoyment of His love. Trust Him to go behind that hole in the wall, or you'll never be free!

Read Mark 12:28,30. What do you think loving God with all your mind means?

____

Loving God with all my mind means asking God to come into secret places. It means trusting that He's not going to reject me or be disgusted with me. He already knows, and He wants in. He cleans up the mind from the inside only.

But we have to cooperate. We apply the principle of feeding what we want to live and starving what we want to die. In other words, we start feeding the Spirit in us and starving the flesh.

Many believers claim what I used to claim: "But I don't feed the flesh." Meanwhile, they watch inappropriate programming, occasional R-rated movies, and engage in impure or unedifying conversation and humor.

The kind of transition I'm describing is radical, but we're living in radical times. The lion wants in the yard; we'd better have a plan to keep him out.

If you haven't already surrendered to the pursuit of loving God with your whole mind and trusting Him to sanctify your thoughts, why not start now? You will be freer and more contented than you've ever been in your life!

Fortified lives: from the walls around our courtyards to the secret, inner courts of the mind. What have you got to lose that's not worth the loss? And just wait until you experience the gain!

In the margin, outline a plan to fortify your life. Do you need to deal with weak or secret places? What things do you need to change?

The Safe House of Love

I got a late start writing today. Toward the end of the praise and worship service I attended in the den of my cabin this morning (by myself), I heard the voice of God speak to my heart: "Come and play." I love that He said, "Come" and not, "Go." "Come." That meant He was already there.

"Love the Lord your God with all your heart and with all your soul and with all your mind and with all your strength" (Mark 12:30).

I also love how I could tell by the sweet tone of the silent voice whispering to my spirit that He was smiling. You know, you can tell that kind of thing in the voices of those you really know. I could have outlined His expression with my finger.

I don't always hear Him like that. Oh, I wish I did, but I don't. Sometimes we have to walk away from the deafening demands of our chaotic lives to inhale His sweet spirit.

We look with pained desperation for things that are already there. Dear Seeker, the breeze is already there. The sunset is already there. The morning tide is already there. The timid doe is already there. The summer rain is already there.

Before going any further in today's lesson, stop for a few moments and go outside. Listen to the sounds God created just for you—the birds chirping, the wind blowing, the rain falling, the leaves crunching under your feet. Notice the colors in the sky, feel the warmth of the sun or the cold and the crisp air against your face. Give thanks to your Creator who created this day. Worship Him.

Describe your worship experience in the margin.

God's love is greater than any earthly love—His true love makes all others seem like shadows. This lavish love of God is meant for every mortal creature who has traveled miles on earth to find a carnal affection that simply suffices.

God waits, watches, and hopes that the sun will not set on our days without our standing on tiptoes at the extremity of life, yelling, "Is there not more than this?" "Ah, yes, my love. There is more."

We sing of this love week after week in our perfectly timed orders of worship while heaven's hosts gather curiously and watch masses of mortals sing in one accord of a love they do not know.

Masses of believers do not realize that love for God is something they can actually feel. In fact, if we don't, we are frighteningly, staggeringly vulnerable to a counterfeit.

I do not suggest that we feel the constant gush of love for God every waking moment any more than I feel the constant gush of love for my husband and children. Yet, my affection for them is a greater reality than my flesh and bone. There are times, however, when I nearly drown in the gush of divine love and marvel that something so full and so perfect could ever come from something so injured as I.

We must neither tolerate a lack of love in our souls nor let anyone convince us that it is normal not to feel love for God. The bride was created to love the Groom. Not only is a lack of love for God our heart's most needless tragedy, but loving God is our only recourse for divinely loving others.

Love is the stuff of intimacy. We can never learn intimacy in even the most anointed corporate worship. We discover divine love in the freedom of solitary confinement with God. We then bring it without so much as a deliberate thought into the great assembly. It simply cannot stay home.

Doctrines of demons will teach you that you can't really find passion in God. They say you cannot really feel spiritual things. They will offer you substitutes, false Christs. "Watch out that no one deceives you. For many will come in my name" (Matt. 24:5). Do not be deceived. It is seduction sent to woo you away from the one thing that is real.

Seek the real with everything in you. More than life. More than breath. More than health. More than blessing. More than gifts. Ask for love. Not just once but over and over for the rest of your days. Ask till your voice is hoarse and with shriveled hand you point to your own aged heart and with one dying word whisper, "More."

Spend time thanking God for His unfailing love for you. Then ask Him for more. He wants to pour out His lavish love on you. Would you let Him?

Write your prayer in the margin.

NOTES

To the Leader:

Spend time this week seeking to love God more. Follow Beth's suggestion to spend some time outside and worship your Creator. A teacher who loves Christ passionately will lead others to seek that kind of love for themselves.

During the Session

1. Ask: *What steps do people take to make their homes safe? Do you think most Christians pay more attention to burglar-proofing their homes or seduce-proofing their lives? Why?* OR Ask those who are parents to detail the steps they took to baby-proof their homes. Ask: *Which of those safeguards were inconvenient or costly? Were they worth it? Why?* FOR EITHER OPTION Explain that it takes effort to seduce-proof our lives against demonic seduction, but doing so can literally save lives.
2. Direct learners to read 1 Thessalonians 5:16-25 in their Bibles and call out ways believers can seduce-proof their lives. Point out that these are all ways to lock the gate when Satan tries to creep into our lives. Ask: *Why aren't some Christians happy in their faith? Why are they vulnerable to seduction?* Invite volunteers to share a difficult time when they could barely force themselves to praise God but did anyway. Ask what resulted from their choice to rejoice always.
3. Discuss how being happy in our faith gives us the power to abstain from evil. Lead the class to describe a pray-without-ceasing relationship with God. Ask: *How does unceasing communication protect us from the enemy? Why is dissatisfaction a stronghold waiting to happen? How does a grateful heart guard against seduction? How do we develop a grateful heart?*
4. Ask what Beth Moore said was most important in seducing-proofing our lives. Remind class members that the Holy Spirit is the only Spirit who can overcome seducing spirits. Ask how effective a home security system is if it is turned off. Explore ways believers turn off or quench the Spirit. Ask why participants agree or disagree that every person needs passion in life. Explain that if we don't allow the Spirit's fire to put passion into our relationship with God, we will find counterfeit passions that will destroy us.
5. Challenge participants to give examples of how someone might despise a warning or instruction and end up taking a major fall. Ask how we can discern whether all teachings and warnings are from God. Explore how a believer can test all things. [Samples: Make sure it's scriptural. Listen

NOTES

to the inner nudgings of the Holy Spirit. Determine how it will affect your witness. Ask yourself whether it will glorify God or yourself.]

6. Turn to Day 1 and discuss the first question (p. 118). Ask why allowing God to set apart every portion of you for Himself will naturally result in the seduce-proofing characteristics you've just discussed. Ask participants to describe the walk and attitude of a seduce-proofed believer. Ask: *Is it easy or difficult to ask others to pray for you? Why? What's the value of enlisting others to pray for you? How can you find these prayer warriors?* Urge participants to ask someone to be an intercessor for them.
7. Lead participants to describe how Satan breaks down our walls of defense against seduction. Ask: *Do you think "Don't sweat the small stuff" is valid advice when it comes to seduce-proofing our lives? Explain. How can the turmoil of everyday life weaken our walls of defense?* Agree that constant battery can wear away at our self-control. Ask someone to read Proverbs 25:28. Ask what happens when we lack self-control. Talk about where we can gain the self-control necessary to keep our walls strong.
8. Discuss the first activity of Day 4 (p. 125). Ask: *What's frightening to you about this passage? You might have answered no when Beth asked if you have a mess behind that hole in the wall, but would you be willing to go a full week with all your thoughts exposed to the public?* Discuss why believers must put forth the constant effort to keep their minds clean. Ask: *In what ways do we feed the flesh and keep that mess behind the wall growing? How can we feed the Spirit and starve these negative thoughts?* Request a volunteer to read Philippians 4:8. Invite the class to give examples of activities that can furnish our minds with pure, noble, and admirable thoughts [urge them to think beyond just "church" things, such as a great ball game, an edifying movie, or musical concert].
9. Discuss the second activity of Day 4 (p. 126). Explore why loving God with your whole being is the ultimate protection. Discuss ways believers can love God more. Invite volunteers to share why they love Christ. Close in prayer.

Wise Up!

Warm Heart, Wise Heads

Our focus this week will be guarding against relational seductions and perhaps a host of other kinds of unhealthy relationships by making sure we are healthy or what the Bible calls sanctified through and through. Keep in mind four important facts to help you avoid making wrong assumptions as we consider this dimension of our study:

1. Seduction does not always involve personal relationships between people. People can be seduced by false doctrine, money, position, power, or any number of secret addictions to things.
2. By no means are all unhealthy relationships demonic seductions.
3. Not all relationships are breeding grounds for seductions. So don't get paranoid and start looking for a demon behind every friend!
4. Relational seduction does not always involve physical or sexual impropriety.

Satan can use relational seduction to promote all kinds of evil, not just those of a sexual nature. He preys upon people's bent toward socialization.

"My prayer is not that you take them out of the world. … As you sent me into the world, I have sent them into the world" (John 17:15,18).

In Matthew 24:12, what did Christ say would happen?

____

What evidence can you see of hearts growing cold in our world today?

____

Examine your own heart. Do you have a coldness of heart toward people in your life? If so, ask God to teach you how to love those people as He loves them.

Christ has called us to stand firm to the end and never give in to a coldness of heart. To Christ, loving was living. The last thing you and I are going to allow the enemy to do is talk us into protecting ourselves from relationally induced seduction by shutting our hearts in a stainless steel box. Disconnection is not an option for followers of Christ. Christ gave His life for people. The Word became flesh for the precise purpose of connecting. Likewise, we have been left on this earth for the unapologetic purpose of connecting with a lost world.

A lot of needy and unhealthy folks are out there. Folks who need ministry. Folks whom Jesus loves. Lives that He wants to redeem. We are His physical body meant to flesh out His ministry to the world, and we can't do our jobs properly or safely if we're not spiritually and emotionally healthy.

The huge irony is this: If we cloister ourselves in the church, we still wouldn't avoid unhealthy relationships. We wouldn't even avoid demonic seductions by shutting out the world and limiting our relationships to those within our church communities. Do you know why? Because so much of it takes place right there.

One of the tricky elements to a relationship Satan has targeted for seduction is that the union may not be with an unbelieving or apparently worldly individual. If Satan wants to seduce a spiritual person, he's often going to use spiritual bait. As we seek to seduce-proof our close relationships within the church community, the goal is godly relationships, not spiritual relationships.

"May God himself, the God of peace, sanctify you through and through. May your whole spirit, soul and body be kept blameless at the coming of our Lord Jesus Christ" (1 Thess. 5:23).

I have heard from few believers in the last several years who were caught in a relational seduction with those they regarded as unbelievers or even those who at first seemed to be prodigal believers. Many of them told me one of the very things that attracted them most was the other person's spirituality. Remember this: Spirituality does not equal godliness in either party nor does being deeply spiritual about Christian things. All sorts of seductions take place in spiritual settings. The point is not to get cynical or suspicious but to get protected and make wise, discerning decisions.

In your own experiences, how has Satan disguised himself? ____________________________________

____

Satan can use believers in all sorts of ways. He simply can't possess them.

One thing we must be warned to avoid at all costs is judging another person's heart. That job is for God and God alone. Judging another's heart, however, is not the same as discerning that something doesn't seem quite right and considering how we might wisely avoid opening ourselves to an intimate or close relationship in the situation.

As people who desire to seduce-proof our lives, we see that the world is going to get increasingly wicked, yet we've been sent smack into the middle of it. We can't even find a guaranteed safe haven in our church communities because relational seductions happen there too.

We are not going to find a guaranteed safe place in which to hide. We are going to have to find safety in Christ, hiding ourselves in Him, no matter what kind of place surrounds us. Anywhere He sends us, He is prepared to protect us.

Sanctified Through and Through

Read John 17:15-18 in the margin. According to these verses what are believers to do?

- ❑ **Seek to become martyrs**
- ❑ **Quarantine ourselves from the world**
- ❑ **Go into the world**

"I do not ask that You will take them out of the world, but that You will keep and protect them from the evil [one]. They are not of the world (worldly, belonging to the world), [just] as I am not of the world. Sanctify them [purify, consecrate, separate them for Yourself, make them holy] by the Truth; Your Word is Truth. Just as You sent Me into the world, I also have sent them into the world (John 17:15-18, AMP).

We have been sent into this world. To disconnect would be in direct disobedience of that purpose. Jesus wants nothing more for His body than our unification. We must stay connected. In both these worlds we need protection from the Evil One. Christ already knew that and petitioned His Father for that very thing. He clearly stated in the passage our means of protection: sanctification.

What does sanctification mean to you?

____

Sanctification is the Holy Spirit's awesome work of setting us apart—purified and consecrated to God—while we're still in troubled settings. Jesus even clearly stated the process of protective sanctification. We are sanctified by the Truth. We are protected from the Evil One when we start allowing, indeed inviting, the Word to penetrate us with its full power and authority.

Much of the body of Christ exists on very little of the actual Word of God. Many of those who get a steady diet of the Word of God don't deliberately receive it (by applying it). We can get truth into our heads without necessarily letting it get to the inner recesses of our minds, literally changing the entire way we process thoughts. Likewise, we often let the Word get to our hearts but don't invite it to take complete residency and authority over our emotions so we can trust some of the things we feel. We say the Word of God is food for our souls, but do we give the Holy Spirit freedom and authority to use it to increasingly transform our entire personalities?

If we are not deliberately asking God to get into every part of our "business," we're not practicing the approach that will protect us. This issue has been the difference between my former and present approach to the Word of God. I loved the Word and studied it feverishly, but the enemy could still have victory over me because I was unknowingly blocking the power and protection of the Word from parts of my life that I either ignored or denied.

I wasn't actively asking God to change the way I think, feel, and perceive. Now I'm a maniac about it. Maybe because I finally realized God's Word was meant for a lot more than I was allowing. These days I want it to the marrow! I don't want a single inch of my body, soul, or spirit to myself. Sanctify it all, Lord Jesus! It's Yours! That's exactly what the Word of God was meant to do.

"The Word that God speaks is alive and full of power [making it active, operative, energizing and effective]; it is sharper than any two-edged sword, penetrating to the dividing line of the breath of life (soul) and [the immortal] spirit, and of joints and marrow [of the deepest parts of our nature], exposing and sifting and analyzing and judging the very thoughts and purposes of the heart. And not a creature exists that is concealed from His sight, but all things are open and exposed, naked and defenseless to the eyes of Him with Whom we have to do. Inasmuch then as we have a great High Priest Who has [already] ascended and passed through the heavens, Jesus the Son of God, let us hold fast our confession [of faith in Him]. For we do not

Take a good look at Hebrews 4:12-16 printed in the margin. Circle the ways the Word of God sanctifies us.

How does it make you feel to know that everything in your life is opened and exposed before God?

❑ **Embarrassed**	❑ **Grateful**	❑ **Condemned**
❑ **Ashamed**	❑ **Peaceful**	❑ **Healed**
❑ **Guilty**	❑ **Unashamed**	❑ **Full of life**

The news that everything in and about our lives is naked and laid bare before God is not meant to terrify His own children. Nor is it meant to make us feel guilty or condemned. These words are meant to tell us that the healing, life-giving, wisdom-rendering power of God's Word reaches every part of us, even the deepest parts of our nature.

If these practices will work for someone who had as much brokenness and defeat as I did, they will work for anyone. God does not play favorites. All He wants us to do is admit our need and welcome Him thoroughly. I believe many Christians are just like I used to be. They are convinced they are allowing the Word to do its sanctifying work simply by partaking of a steady diet of sermons and Bible studies. They even love the Word. Still, they may have unknowingly practiced such selective application that some places remain unprotected. No need to wait until something painful happens. You can change your approach today!

Start practicing an open dialogue with God concerning your past, present, and future. Talk candidly to Him concerning weaknesses, temptations, and tendencies to sin. Ask Him to reveal any area of your life that you may be unknowingly keeping under lock and key from the reaching, healing power of His Word. Approach God as your daily counselor who knows you better than you know yourself. Not only will you find protection, you will discover a level of intimacy with Him unlike anything you've ever experienced.

We've got a world out there that needs the ministry Christ has assigned to us. We've got a body of believers to love and serve. We don't want to be accidents waiting to happen in either of those important fields. Let's allow God to have His unhindered way with every part of us.

have a High Priest Who is unable to understand and sympathize and have a shared feeling with our weaknesses and infirmities and liability to the assaults of temptation, but One Who has been tempted in every respect as we are, yet without sinning. Let us then fearlessly and confidently and boldly draw near to the throne of grace (the throne of God's unmerited favor to us sinners), that we may receive mercy [for our failures] and find grace to help in good time for every need [appropriate help and well-timed help, coming just when we need it]" (Heb. 4:12-16, AMP).

Clean Ties

Those of us who have received Christ Jesus as our personal Savior have received the Holy Spirit. We have been made clean by the sanctifying work of the Holy Spirit. He moved into us, bringing His cleanness with Him.

Satan knows that God wants to present His Son with a pure, spotless, virgin bride, so he's doing everything he can to defile her. What he doesn't seem to get is that he cannot touch or taint the Spirit of Christ in us, which is what ultimately gives us our pure standing before God.

"Flee from sexual immorality. All other sins a man commits are outside his body, but he who sins sexually sins against his own body" (1 Cor. 6:18).

If Satan can't make us unclean, he will do everything he can to make us feel unclean. He knows that our unclean feelings can eventually cause us to act unclean. Our defense is to form close relationships. When I use the word *clean*, I ask you to translate the word more widely than that which is opposed to *filthy*. I ask you to translate the word *clean* as opposed to *messy*.

What would be the difference between *filthy* and

***messy*? ____**

Let me explain why our definition is critical. Many ties aren't clean that don't necessarily fall under the category of *filthy*. A relationship doesn't have to be dirty to be unhealthy and/or seductive. It can simply be *messy*. We'll adopt the meaning of *messy* as the antithesis of *clean* according to its definitions in *Merriam Webster's Collegiate Dictionary*: "marked by confusion, disorder, or dirt ... careless, slovenly ... extremely unpleasant or trying."

Have you ever been in a messy relationship?
❑ Yes ❑ No If yes, describe briefly in the margin.

The word *clean* encompasses a broader meaning than the opposite of filthy. Most Christians stereotype any kind of sexual sin as dirty, but we can find ourselves in a seductive mess that never gets physical. Let's go ahead and discuss sexual seduction to some degree first. Then in our next lesson we'll broaden our thinking to include other kinds of messy relationships.

Remember that sexual sin can be virtually unmatched in its destructive and addictive power. Unhealthy sexuality is an extremely blatant target for seduction. We established earlier that not all unhealthy relationships are the specific targets of demonic seduction. However, every assault on the believer's life to get him or her involved in an extramarital sexual relationship is seduction. My grounds for such a categorization is the Book of Proverbs, which labels the tempter to sexual sin a seducer or seductress.

Read Proverbs 7 and list ways this man was seduced.

____

____

Perhaps the only positive thing about sexual seduction is that we can recognize it better than some other forms of relational seduction. We must learn to form neater and cleaner ties. An extramarital tie of any kind has lost its cleanness and neatness the moment any level of sexuality enters into it.

Countless adults enter into sexual sin through elicit conversation, off-color teasing, flirting, and inappropriate demonstrations of affection. As long as they don't commit fornication, they rationalize that they really haven't done anything wrong.

Any sign of relating sexually to anyone besides our marriage partner signals a demonic scheme of seduction. I believe that includes any intrusion into the thought life or what the world calls the fantasy life. The Word of God uses a very strong command for times when we're tempted to sexual immorality.

Write in BIG letters the first word of 1 Corinthians 6:18.

____

Scripture tells us to run for our lives from sexual sin. Recently I talked with a believer who has been caught in a scheme with a neighbor. If the situation is not diffused immediately, one of them needs to move. The same is true of a budding extramarital relationship at work. If it can't be diffused without delay, someone needs to change jobs. That's what God means when He says, "Flee!"

If the believer has already been caught in the web of seduction, he or she may feel a diminished power to run. What should that believer do? Tell someone in godly authority whom he or she can trust! Remember, Satan loves a secret! You diffuse the scheme when you divulge the secret to someone who can help you through prayer and strict accountability.

Relating romantically is not the same thing as relating sexually. Godly young couples who are not yet married can relate romantically with a sweet innocence, but even they need to be careful to avoid crossing what can be a fine line of relating sexually. They have to be all the more careful not to give the enemy a foothold.

Satan would do anything to counterfeit the gift of sexuality God gave to a man and wife. Nothing is any cleaner. Let's guard the precious gift we've been given.

Beware of the Web

"Since we are surrounded by such a great cloud of witnesses, let us throw off everything that hinders and the sin that so easily entangles, and let us run with perseverance the race marked out for us" (Heb. 12:1).

In our last lesson we discussed sexual seduction. Today I want us to consider some examples of nonsexual relational seduction.

I have a dear friend who along with her husband was caught in the powerful seduction of a religious cult. They were very active Christians who were enticed by a church that professed to practices very close to those of the early church in the Book of Acts. In actuality very few of their practices ended up imitating the early church with the convenient exception of pooled finances. They did not realize how far they were veering from the Word into man-induced legalism and bondage because the leaders interpreted the Scripture for them. They were not encouraged to study the Bible for themselves. Are you beginning to recognize the signs? They lost the active protection of the ongoing sanctification of God's truth.

This family was seduced into losing practically everything they had except their salvation and one another. My friend testifies that this cult had a terrifying seductive power to control the mind and blind the eyes. The hardest part of the cult to walk away from was the closeness of the members Their lives were extremely intertwined. Their ties were not sexual, but they were messy.

Let's address one more example of nonsexual relational seduction in hopes that you'll have enough information to recognize the messy lines that put relationships at risk.

What did Jesus warn us about in Matthew 24:4-5?

____

Read 2 Corinthians 11:4-6. What did the Apostle Paul imply about the message others were preaching?

____

Anyone who becomes a "Christ" to us constitutes an ungodly tie no matter how spiritual he or she may be. Whether or not the person intentionally solicits dependency and devotion, Satan's scheme is to subtly transfer the deep devotion the believer has felt to Christ to a mortal instead.

Have you ever had anyone in your life who became a "Christ" to you? ❑ Yes ❑ No If yes, how did you develop such dependency on this person?

___

Any relationship in which we begin to emotionally attribute some of the biblically specified activities of Christ to a person is not only an unhealthy tie, it is a mess. God will not share His glory with another. He will neither bless nor tolerate someone becoming a savior to us.

Remember when I listed the common claims of the seduced? I pointed out that many caught in relational seductions used the word *web* to describe them.

Hebrews 12:1 says that sin "entangles us." Sinful relationships are entangling relationships. We have discussed sexually relational seductions and nonsexually relational seductions. All had messy ties as opposed to the clean ties that protect the believer from seduction. All of them formed sinful entanglements. Whether we call it a web or an entanglement, the relationship lacks the clean, uncomplicated lines of godliness.

How can we keep our relational ties healthy and clean? Keep Christ between them! Although we are imperfect people and we will always be challenged by imperfect relationships, I think the lines of the cross between us can offer a plumb line that can become a constant goal.

What if we're willing to respect clean lines in our relationships but others in the relationship are not? We can't change anyone else. We can't even change ourselves! But we can allow God to change us. As we determine to allow God to manage our relationships, we leave Christ to tangle with them instead of us. And, guess what? He can handle them. No amount of ties can bind Him. That's not true of any of the rest of us. Give Him the ropes.

Pray for the strength and courage to do what you must do in order to be obedient to God.

See-Through Lives

Christ is returning for a pure bride who will be living in the most impure world in human history. Her purity will not develop accidentally. As wickedness increases, our only wise recourse is to increase our pursuit of God and godliness all the more.

"Let us consider and give attentive, continuous care to watching over one another, studying how we may stir up (stimulate and incite) to love and helpful deeds and noble activities, not forsaking or neglecting to assemble together [as believers], as is the habit of some people, but admonishing (warning, urging and encouraging) one another, and all the more faithfully as you see the day approaching" (Heb. 10:24-25, AMP).

Hebrews 10:24-25 addresses a vital method of increasing our fortification. Read this passage in the margin. Underline how we are to respond to other believers.

This Scripture is talking about deliberately involving ourselves with one another for aiding and abetting each other's victories. Warning, urging, and encouraging one another. Those who isolate themselves from the involvement of the body of Christ will be at great risk for personal disaster.

Some Christians are so watchful of others that they don't watch over themselves. They see specks in others' eyes and miss the planks in their own. That's not the kind of thing the writer of Hebrews is talking about. His exhortation is about love, helpfulness, and nobility between believers. These verses are about encouraging one another and watching out for one another.

We have a responsibility to one another to (1) develop and practice godly discernment and (2) develop and practice deliberate accountability.

Discernment does not mean a critical or judgmental spirit. Embodied in the concept of discernment is the ability to see through what may not be obvious to the eye. Discernment sees trouble, senses a warning, and cites the need for caution. We can't trust what we're sensing in the spirit if we're not filled with the Holy Spirit.

What does Hebrews 3:13 say we are to do daily?

____

Why? ____________________________________

What do we do if to the best of our understanding we are filled by the Holy Spirit and we sense something is wrong with a fellow believer? First, we spend serious time in prayer! God may desire that we make a loving approach at an appropriate time just to say we've had him or her on our minds and ask if everything is all right. Then leave the results up to the Holy Spirit.

God has never failed to bring someone into my path who discerns when something is wrong. Often God may appoint a person I'd never suspect. Sometimes our discernment can be clouded by strong feelings in closer relationships, but it works with startling clarity around those with whom we are a little less emotionally involved.

Is there someone in your life right now who you discern is struggling in a situation? Write his or her initials here _________ and begin to pray. Ask God to show you when and how to approach this person.

A second suggestion for helping one another responsibly involves developing and practicing accountability. If we're going to be fortified against seduction, you and I need a small group of people we invite to hold us accountable to the pursuit of godliness. Accountability partners mean individuals we invite to see through us. Only those who are willing to be vulnerable will experience the protection accountability can bring.

We want to choose our accountability partners prayerfully and soberly under the leadership of the Holy Spirit. Those we ask to hold us accountable should be people we deeply respect and who have proved trustworthy over a length of time. (Beware of instant intimacy with anyone! Instant intimacy is one of the leading warning signals of a seduction!)

"I am jealous for you with a godly jealousy. I promised you to one husband, to Christ, so that I might present you as a pure virgin to him. But I am afraid that just as Eve was deceived by the serpent's cunning, your minds may somehow be led astray from your sincere and pure devotion to Christ" (2 Cor. 11:2-3).

Read 2 Corinthians 11:2-3 printed in the margin and underline descriptions of godly accountability.

Paul left no doubt in his letter to the Corinthians. He intended to hold them accountable to godliness. He had a godly jealousy for their best.

See-through lives. That's what we need. Whether we realize it or not, you and I are desperate for people who can see through our lives. With their help, we can begin practicing lives of inside-out veracity that anybody can see through.

Discernment: the ability to see through the masks
Accountability: inviting others to see through us
Both help us see this faith thing through with integrity.

NOTES

To the Leader:

Examine your ties to people—particularly class participants. Are they clean ties? Is there any messiness there? Is someone becoming too dependent on you? Is there an undercurrent that's not quite right? Do whatever you must do to put Christ between all your relationships. Be sure to let your participants know how much you love and appreciate them.

Before the Session

Obtain a rope if you are using the second option in step 1 and a loaf of bread for step 3.

During the Session

1. Ask: *What's the difference between a godly relationship and a spiritual relationship? Which relationship should you seek and which should you avoid? Why?* OR Invite two volunteers to stand side by side. Wrap the rope around them; then ask them to untangle themselves. Ask how the demonstration illustrates some relationships. FOR EITHER OPTION Explain: *We must wise up so Satan won't use our God-given bent toward socialization to entangle us. Today's goal is to determine how to avoid seductive relationships.*
2. Discuss the first activity of Day 1 (p. 131). Ask why believers might develop cold hearts in a wicked world. Request that learners read John 17:15,18 and discuss why disconnection from this world is not an option. Ask: *Is the church a safe place to develop relationships? Why?* Read 1 Thessalonians 5:23 in the margin (p. 132) and state how believers can have warm hearts yet wise heads in developing relationships in the world and the church.
3. Explore the meaning of sanctification. Ask what sanctifies believers. Ask: *Many Christians are exposed to the Word through attending church and Bible studies; are they sanctified and protected from seductive relationships? Why?* Display the loaf of bread. Explain: *We can discuss the bread, remark how beautiful, delicious, and life-giving the bread is, and perhaps even nibble the bread. But what happens if we never put forth the effort to bite off, chew, and swallow that bread?* Explain that without sustenance people would soon grow weak. Ask learners to recall on whom Satan preys. Discuss the Hebrews 4:12-16 activity in Day 2 (p. 134). Encourage: *Don't just let the Word get to you—let it go through and through you! How can we really eat this Bread so it sets apart every aspect of ourselves for God?*
4. Ask which participants like a little mess and why. Ask: *When it comes to relationships is "messy" ever positive? Why?* Discuss the first question

NOTES

in Day 3 (p. 136). Guide the class to explore Proverbs 7 to discover how the young man got roped into a messy and dirty relationship. Discuss what Beth Moore said was the only positive thing about sexual seduction. Ask: *According to 1 Corinthians 6:18, what must we do when even a hint of sexuality enters into any extramarital relationship?* Request the class describe real-life ways a believer might need to flee from a seductive relationship.

5. Remind the class that in Day 4 Beth Moore discussed two examples of nonsexual relational messes: unhealthy dependency on others and allowing someone to become a false Christ to us. Ask participants to describe relationships that fit those two categories. Request that someone read Job 8:13-15. Lead the class to compare seductive relationships to a spider web. Ask: *Do you intentionally walk into a spider's web? What happens when you do? How can we guard against unintentionally wandering into sticky, messy relationships?* Invite volunteers to share how they have discerned that something wasn't quite right in a relationship and what they did about it.
6. Draw two stick figures on the board with a rope entangling them. Ask if that kind of entangling relationship makes those two figures stronger or weaker and why. Draw two more stick figures on the board. Draw a cross between them with the horizontal line touching each figure. Ask: *How are these persons connected? Does this kind of connectedness make them stronger or weaker? Why? How does the cross provide appropriate boundaries?* Explain that when we keep Christ between our relationships, we are freed from messy ties. If the other person in the relationship doesn't want to let go of the ropes, let God deal with that person; you stay on the side of the cross.
7. Ask: *If relationships can get so messy and complicated, wouldn't we be better off avoiding all relationships? Why?* Discuss the first two activities in Day 5 (p. 140). Lead the class to share practical ways believers can encourage and stir one another to good deeds. Ask participants to define accountability and explain why believers need it. Discuss the final activity of Day 5. Explore why a best friend might not be the best choice for an accountability partner and how participants can find the right believers to hold them accountable. Encourage participants to ensure that all their relational ties are clean. Close the session in prayer.

The Way Home

Name Calling

" 'Come now, let us reason together,' says the LORD. 'Though your sins are like scarlet, they shall be as white as snow; though they are red as crimson, they shall be like wool' " (Isa. 1:18).

During the final two weeks of our journey together we will discover precepts in Scripture that will guide us to hope and restoration. Today's lesson will be different from the rest. It contains my story. Perhaps you can relate or you know someone who can. I ask you to read it prayerfully and then spend time reflecting on your own life. If you can't relate, but know someone who can, pray for that person and his or her restoration.

My name is Had. You may know me, but you may not know my new name. You may have no idea what I've been through because I do my best to look the same. I am scared to death of you. I used to be just like you. I once held my head up high without propping it on my hymnal.

I was well respected back then, and I even respected myself. I was wholeheartedly devoted to God, and if the truth be known, somewhere deep inside I was sometimes the slightest bit proud of my devotion. Then I'd repent ... because I knew pride was wrong. I didn't want to be wrong. Not ever.

People looked up to me. And life looked good from up there. I felt good about who I was. That was before I was Had. Strangely, I no longer remember my old name. I just remember I liked it. I liked who I was. I wish I could go back. I wish I'd just wake up. But I fear I'm wide awake. I have had a nightmare. And the nightmare was me. Had.

If I could really talk to you and you could really listen, I'd tell you I have no idea how all this happened. Honestly, I was just like you. I didn't plan to be Had. I didn't want to be Had. One day I hadn't, then the next day I had.

Oh, I know now where I went wrong. I have rewound the nightmare a thousand times, stopping it right at the point where I departed the trail of good sense. The way ahead didn't look wrong. It just looked different. Strange, he didn't look like the Devil in the original scene. But every time I replayed it, he dropped another piece of his masquerade. When he finally took off his mask, he was laughing at me. Nothing seems funny anymore. I will never laugh again as long as he is laughing.

If only I could go back, I would see it this time! I would walk around the trap camouflaged by the brush, and I would not be Had. I would be Proud. Was that my old name? Proud? I can't even remember who I was anymore. I thought I was Good. Not Proud. But I don't know anymore.

Would you believe I never heard the trap shut? Too many voices were shouting in my head. I just knew I got stuck somewhere unfamiliar, and soon I didn't like the scenery anymore. I wanted to go home. My ankle didn't even hurt at first. Not until the infection set in. Then I thought I would die.

I lay like a whimpering doe while the wolf howled in the darkness. I got scared. I pulled the brush over me and hid. Then I felt like I couldn't breathe. I had to get out of there or I was sure it would kill me. I didn't belong there. I refused to die there.

I pulled and pulled at the trap, but the foothold wouldn't budge. The blood gushed. I had no way out. I screamed for God. I told Him where I was and the shape I was in. He came for me.

The infection is gone. He put something on it and cleaned it up instantly. As He inspected my shattered ankle, I kept waiting for Him to say, "You deserved this, you know. You've been Had." Because I did and I know and I have. He hasn't said it yet. I don't know whether He will or not. I don't know how much to trust Him yet. I've never known Him from this side. My leg still hurts. God says it will heal with time. But I fear I will always walk with a limp.

You see, I wrestled with the Devil and he gave me a new name. Had.

Have you ever been Had? ❑ Yes ❑ No
If so, describe your experience in the margin.

If you have never been Had, do you really think it is possible? ❑ Yes ❑ No ❑ Not sure

Why? ____

God says He doesn't want me to forget. He wants to make sure I never act like I haven't been Had, so He left the scars. He kept a set on His own hands and feet and left one on my ankle. That's OK. My scars bear the marks of death. Don't let anyone tell you that being Had won't kill you. It will. It was meant to. If it doesn't, you've been Had for nothing and you'll be Had again.

Perhaps we all need to know how it feels to be dead for a while. But do we believe we might see the glory of God? That's what Christ told Martha she would see. When He raised Lazarus from the dead, Christ did not raise Him sick. He raised him healed. I have a suspicion that Lazarus never got to kid himself into thinking he couldn't get sick again.

What lessons can you take from today's study?

___

If you don't really relate to some of the material this week, give thanks to God. You can still read and study to understand and support some people who do.

Starting Home

"Godly sorrow brings repentance that leads to salvation and leaves no regret, but worldly sorrow brings death" (2 Cor. 7:10).

This week we are going to discover ways to start the journey toward home. Very likely you are somewhere between having a thousand feelings and having none at all. That's OK.

Your heart has been so misshapen by the twists of Satan's lies that you'd better not trust it for a while. You'll know when your heart is starting to get well. It will hurt so badly with throbbing pangs of repentance, you'll think you're going to die. And you will. Then God will raise you from the very thing that has been the death of you. He really will give you a future.

Satan wants you to feel hopeless. He is a liar. You belong to God. You are His and nothing has ripped you from His hand. To remind you of that, take a pen right now and write in the margin several times: "I am God's."

Because you know it's your only ticket to freedom, chain yourself to the wrist of Christ and start taking your first steps out of the darkness. You probably don't trust anyone right now, and you're not even sure you can trust God. You can, but you'll learn all that for yourself. No one can really tell you what you're about to learn for yourself—if you're willing.

Don't worry about the future right now. Just offer Him your wrist and tell Him to drag you home even if you're not sure you belong or even want to go. You do. You're just too wounded to feel it.

What will God do because of His blood covenant with you (Zech. 9:11-12)?

____

I want to ask you to muster up every bit of courage within you and ask God to baptize you in a tide of sorrow over your sin. Ask Him to do it for as long as necessary until full repentance comes.

Don't be afraid of this kind of sorrow. The Bible calls this "godly sorrow" (2 Cor. 7:10), and it is the most wonderful thing that can happen to you in the next little while. You cannot be restored until it comes.

Don't misunderstand. I don't want you waiting on this sorrow to come before you walk away from your darkness. Often you have to walk away from the seductive clutches of the Evil One to begin feeling godly sorrow.

Ask Christ to come get you. Then ask the Holy Spirit who has been temporarily quenched to come and do His job. Be patient until He does. The tide may come in slowly, but if you belong to God, it will come. It must.

Better to admit where you're not and ask God's help to get you where you need to be. Do not fake a manifestation of the Spirit that isn't there. Have no confidence in your flesh. Just be real before Him. That's what He wants from you. That's what He wants from all of us.

To some who were confident of their own righteousness and looked down on everybody else, Jesus told a parable.

Read Luke 18:10-14. What was the difference in the ways the Pharisee and the tax collector prayed?

____

What point did Jesus make in this parable?

___

That's what Christ is looking for as you find your way back. The way home is humility. Make no excuses. Rationalize nothing. Blame no one. Humble yourself. If you don't yet feel the sorrow that you know will be necessary, ask God for it like a beggar asks for bread. Humble yourself, dear one. Come in total weakness to Him.

In the verses below, underline what James 4:9-10 tells us to do.

"Grieve, mourn and wail. Change your laughter to mourning and your joy to gloom. Humble yourselves before the Lord, and he will lift you up."

God wants us to humble ourselves, but He also wants to lift us up! Anyone who has been wholeheartedly, sincerely, and purely devoted to Christ and yet has gone through the horror of seduction will come out of it with a humility that can last a lifetime. God forgives and forgets because He does not need to remember. We are forgiven, but do not forget because we are wise never to lose sight of where we've been and how God has rescued us.

"We are forgiven, but do not forget because we are wise never to lose sight of where we've been and how God has rescued us." —Beth Moore

Had, here's the deal. You will never be able to go back to Have Not. Proud is totally out of the question, and "*No one* is good—except God alone" (Luke 18:19, emphasis mine). But you can go forward with what Hads can have. You can have an extra dose of humility. You can have a fresh wave of gratitude. And you can have a growth spurt of grace. So can every other believer, but somehow Hads may be a little more likely to feel grateful. It's up to you.

A Path of Hope and Restoration

Why the small group of us had the audacity to sit around and discuss a brother's life, especially one we had never met, is a mystery to me. But that's what we did. A Christian singer who had ministered to tens of thousands had tumbled headlong into a fall. I only know that because he said it of himself.

This singer had admitted his sin, and as if the pain he was suffering were not enough, the Christian world began casting their votes as to whether he should ever be allowed to sing Christian music again. I cannot find a single time in Scripture when God called upon the popular vote of people to help Him deliver a verdict over one of His children. Goodness knows, most of the population would be condemned to the fiery reaches by now.

"The LORD said to Samuel, 'Do not consider his appearance or his height, for I have rejected him. The LORD does not look at the things man looks at. Man looks at the outward appearance, but the LORD looks at the heart' " (1 Sam. 16:7).

According to 1 Samuel 16:7, how does God make His decisions? ____________________________________

God does not look on the outward appearance of things. He makes His decisions based on what He sees in the heart. God knows things we don't know. He looks upon the heart. And, by the way, He doesn't take very kindly to people telling Him how to do His job.

I went to bed that night very disturbed. I tossed and turned as I thought about my own tumultuous young life and how much grace and patience God had shown me as He taught—and was still teaching—me to walk on legs that had been handicapped for a very long time. I wondered, *Have I come just a half a cup short of all the grace I'm going to get? Is there a limited supply?* If so, I felt rather like David in Psalm 101:2 when he confidently announced to God, "I will be careful to lead a blameless life." Then, as if he considered about how long he thought he could keep it up, he followed his vow with the words, "When will you come to me?"

I think maybe David thought he could keep it up until sundown if God wouldn't mind coming to get him before dinner. I thought of countless others who were like me and had required a generous helping of second chances to learn how to keep their wagons between the ditches. None of us had been so "blessed" with a public trial as our popular brother.

I brought all sorts of questions before the Lord. "Am I that off base? Am I just softhearted because I have been such a grace project myself? Have I lost my balance? Did I ever have any? I know he needs help and could really use a break, but is he a castaway in evangelical America?

I understand some must take the hard line and make it tough for people to come back again so they will not take the grace of God lightly. I do believe people in the spotlight have a major responsibility regarding the body of Christ. I also believe in discipline and have been on the other end of God's chastising rod more than a few times. I believe in repentance, the real kind. The radical kind. Still, this side of the fence is where I belong. I would be nothing less than a hypocrite if I refused a brother and sister the right to draw from the bottomless well of God's grace and try again. I had to learn to swim in grace to live.

List in the margin some personal experiences where you deserved judgment but instead God showered you with His grace.

First Samuel 12:20-25 represents some of the clearest orderly concepts for restoration. We will give them much attention over the next few days and in the next lesson. May God take them and walk you through them with Spirit-filled comprehension. May they become a path of clarity and hope to you.

We will take each precept individually, considering how it applies to New Testament believers. We don't have to make any big reaches for application. Israel's situation was conceptually identical to someone being seduced from his or her wholehearted, sincere, and pure devotion to God for lesser—even spiritual or earthly acceptable—things. God's people are neither to be like the world and take on the habits of surrounding pagans nor ever to allow something that even seems spiritual or reasonable to disconnect us from the Head (see Col. 2:19).

Our God of inconceivable grace and patience did not leave them or us without remedy. The very fact that He inspired it to be written into Scripture means it has something to say to us. With this foundation poured, we'll begin going through each precept of the prescription God wrote His children through His prophet Samuel.

Trekking with Facts, Not Fear

First Samuel 12:20-25 provides a road map for restoration. We are going to examine each phrase to see what facts we can learn about restoration.

"Do not be afraid" (v. 20). When we've really been Had and we're beginning to wake up to what is happening, one of the first, most inundating waves of emotion is fear. I find it interesting and infuriating that Satan subtly talks people into things and then proceeds to taunt and terrorize them with fear.

The enemy can fuel fear through three primary areas: fear of consequences, fear of people, and fear of future circumstances.

"God planned before time to present His Son through a royal line. 'The LORD is my light and my salvation—whom shall I fear? The LORD is the stronghold of my life—of whom shall I be afraid?' " (Ps. 27:1).

Have you ever experienced fear in any of these areas?
❑ Yes ❑ No If so, which ones and how?

____

____

You probably have never been in a position where you were forced to trust totally in the sovereignty of God. You will either learn to trust Him as never before, or you will be impaired for the rest of your life. He will not appoint any chastisement or allow any consequences that cannot be used for your ultimate benefit.

Enlist prayer warriors to start praying for you. Together start binding the enemy from any further work in your situation. Ask God to bind Satan and to loose the Holy Spirit on every single detail.

Read Matthew 18:19-20. What did Jesus say happens

when we pray together? ______________________

As you and several others agree in binding the enemy, whatever is loosed, even if it is temporarily painful, will work for your good.

Completely humble and surrender yourself and all things concerning you into God's loving hands and His wise plan.

You may be tempted to worry about what people are saying. You're going to have to release them and your pride entirely to the Lord. You may even have to let go of your overwhelming desire to take up for yourself if gossipers share things they don't even know.

Seek God's approval with everything in you, and ask for the empowering of His Spirit not to let your sin make you a servant of men.

"You have done all this evil" (v. 20). Dealing with the evil we have done is one of the most critical parts of the process. Do not downplay the seriousness of any sin you have committed. Do not give in to the temptation to transfer your sin, blame it, or rationalize it.

Whatever your circumstances, if you have been seduced away from your wholehearted, sincere, and pure devotion to Christ, something huge has happened, and sin has been involved. The more seriously you take the seduction, the more freedom God will have to deal with it fully and get your precious life back on track.

The closer you have been to God, the more sensitive you are likely to be to all kinds of offenses. Even if others don't see the big deal, if you have been close enough to God to know it is a big deal, you are wise to make a very big deal of it with Him and whomever else you must to be fully restored. This kind of confession and willingness to take full responsibility will prove to be life to you and the full catalyst of forgiveness and restoration.

"*Yet do not turn away from the Lord*" (v. 20). Whatever way you've been Had and no matter what you have done, please don't even consider turning away from the Lord as an option. That's what the enemy is after!

Of the three precepts we studied today, which one is the most difficult for you?

- ❑ **Trusting God instead of living in fear**
- ❑ **Confessing my sin before God and, when necessary, before others**
- ❑ **Believing God to forgive my sins and cleanse me from all unrighteousness**

What do you really believe about God? What you are going through right now is going to help you answer that question. You may be about to find out that some or much of what you've believed wasn't nearly enough or that it wasn't even accurate. Was your faith in yourself and in your ability to be good, righteous, and always wise? or was your faith in God? If your faith is in your own righteousness, you are in big trouble.

The Word is clear that the work of the cross is finished. The means of forgiveness and total purification for every sin we have or will ever commit and obediently confess has already been accomplished. Are we going to have faith in God and His Word or in our ridiculously weak and sin-prone selves?

Keep on Trekking

Today we continue to look at precepts from 1 Samuel 12:20-25. Before we delve into God's Word, take a moment to pray—ask God to open your heart and mind to receive what He has for you today.

"Being confident of this, that he who began a good work in you will carry it on to completion until the day of Christ Jesus" (Phil. 1:6).

"Serve the Lord with all your heart" (v. 20). I do not believe God wills for the body of Christ to refuse a seduced servant who has been wholeheartedly, sincerely, and purely devoted to Christ the right to serve again. You may as well hang him with a rope because you will virtually kill him.

They need to seek sound spiritual and emotional health, but the goal must be fully restored servants of Jesus Christ. The type of service may need to change, but to refuse the right to serve at all is nearly to destroy them.

I don't even think those who have never been wholeheartedly devoted and end up falling in their own rebellion ought to be refused the right to serve after complete repentance and an active pursuit toward spiritual wellness. Their failure may be the very thing God uses to sift them and make them true foot-washing servants.

The truly repentant are often so purified and humbled by disaster that they are willing to do anything! If persons who claim repentance are still arrogant and unwilling to take responsibility, they are probably missing the fruit of repentance. They are a long way from ready, but don't bail on them! Help them, speak the truth in love, and pray them to true repentance!

In Scripture, if Christians had gone too far ever to serve again, God usually struck them dead and took them home. Just ask Ananias and Sapphira (Acts 5). If the believer is still living and bears fruit of repentance, I do not believe God is finished using hiim or her to serve Him in some way. Seek the wisdom of God!

What does Galatians 6:1 say we are to do to someone caught in sin? ________________________________

No Christian in his or her right mind would say a repentant Had couldn't be forgiven by God or shouldn't be forgiven by others. The controversy seems to concern what Had is allowed to do even after he is healed.

First Samuel 12:20 says not to turn away from the Lord; instead serve Him with all your heart. Likely, the very issue in some Hads' lives who lacked complete devotion might have been that they were not serving with all their hearts. Part of their prescription would be to return to serving God—but this time with all their hearts.

The Lord will not reject you no matter what you've done to your name. His faithfulness to you is based on His great name! His great name stands even if we fall!

"For the sake of his great name the LORD will not reject his people" (1 Sam 12:22).

"The LORD was pleased to make you his own" (1 Sam. 12:22). Not only are you protected from rejection for the sake of God's great name, it just so happens that the Lord was pleased to make you His own.

The Lord rescued you because He delighted in you. He who began a good work will be faithful to complete it (Phil. 1:6).

"In love he predestined us to be adopted as his sons through Jesus Christ, in accordance with his pleasure and will. ... In him we have redemption through his blood, the forgiveness of sins, in accordance with the riches of God's grace that he lavished on us with all wisdom and understanding. In him we were also chosen, having been predestined according to the plan of him who works out everything in conformity with the purpose of his will" (Eph. 1:4-5,7-8,11).

Read the Ephesians passage printed in the margin. Underline the privileges that are ours through Christ.

The same mind who knew in advance you would become one of His children also knew in advance you'd fall for a deceptive scheme of the Evil One. Still, He says you were adopted with pleasure.

Please hear this with your whole heart. When you say, "God, thank You so much for saving me and making me Your child." According to Scripture He doesn't just say, "You're welcome." Hear Him say, "It was My pleasure."

God lavishes His grace on you with all wisdom and understanding. He's not running low. God will work this out, dear Had, in conformity with the purpose of His will. You haven't done the one thing God can't turn around and use together with everything else in your life for good.

Whether you are a Had or a Have Not, read Psalm 139:23-24 below and make it your prayer.

"Search me, O God, and know my heart; test me and know my anxious thoughts. See if there is any offensive way in me, and lead me in the way everlasting."

During the Session

1. Ask: *What's the farthest you've ever been from home? How long did it take you to return home? How did you feel when got there?* OR Ask: *Have you ever been Had?* Invite volunteers to share practical jokes that have been played on them or others. Explain that being Had by Satan is no joke. Every Christian has the potential to be Had by Satan, but they'll never stop being Held by their Father.
2. Invite volunteers to share how they felt about "Had" from Day 1 and why. Ask: *Do you ever wish you could run and hide from God? When?* Invite someone to read Psalm 139:7-10. Explain: *When you fail God, it's impossible to run and hide from Him, so you might as well run home. Today we'll discover ways to start the journey home.* Write "I am God's" on the board. Instruct participants to write that phrase in the margin of their books if they haven't already and then turn and declare it to the person next to them. Ask: *Why is it vital to remind ourselves of that truth as we begin our journey home?*
3. Guide the class to find and read Zechariah 9:11-12 in their Bibles. Lead a discussion with: *How are those who have been seduced described? Where have they been living? What will God do for them? How can those who have been Had return to God's fortress?* To answer that last question share that we must: *1. Ask for godly sorrow; 2. Be patient and self-motivated* (discuss the role of both in returning home); *and 3. Humble ourselves.* Discuss the final activity of Day 2. Ask: *If God forgives and forgets, why doesn't He allow us to forget when we've really blown it?* Acknowledge that remembering our failure can actually protect us from further seduction. But we must forgive ourselves and go forward. Ask participants to read the final paragraph of Day 2 (p. 148) and discuss what Christians who have been Had can take with them as they move forward.
4. Discuss the first activity of Day 3. Explore why that is good news for Christians who have fallen and a warning for those who haven't. Ask participants if they've ever received God's grace when they deserved judgment. Ask: *Are we more likely to give grace or judgment to fellow believers who have fallen?* Explain that the steps to restoration discussed in this

NOTES

To the Leader:

If you've ever been Had (seduced by the enemy), examine how that experience has actually made you a better teacher. Thank God for restoring you and using that terrible experience for good in your life. If you've never been Had, thank God and ask Him to continue protecting you. Request a special measure of grace and understanding to gently restore and encourage those in your class who have been Had and are seeking to return.

NOTES

week's study are an encouragement to those who need to return home and a challenge to those Christians who have never been seduced.

5. Ask class members to follow along in their Bibles as someone reads 1 Samuel 12:19-25. Ask them how Israel sinned. Remind them we will be seduced anytime we allow anything other than the King to rule over us. Ask what they find interesting about the first thing God declared to His fallen people. Discuss what we're most likely to be afraid of after we've fallen. Examine what we must do with our fear.
6. Ask how the Israelites demonstrated godly sorrow. Discuss how believers can acknowledge the seriousness of their sin. Ask why we might want to turn from God when we fail Him. Share that a time of seduction will force Christians to examine what they really believe about the Lord. Urge: *You've got to believe that He is enough to cover all your sin—His death was enough, His grace is enough, and His power is enough to bring you home.*
7. Ask what God wants all believers, even those who have been seduced, to do according to 1 Samuel 12:24. Ask: *How can those who have been Had actually serve God better than they did before? How can church leaders demonstrate grace and wisdom in restoring Christians to service in the church?*
8. Discuss the second activity of Day 5 (p. 154). Ask: *In whom do you delight and why? Can you begin to believe God feels that way about you? How can that truth give the seduced believer the courage to head back home?* Ask parents how they feel about people criticizing or punishing their children. Ask: *How do you think God feels when His church criticizes or punishes His children in whom He delights?* Exhort: *If you've been Had, head home. If you've never been Had, help those who have to make it back home.* Use the final activity of Day 5 as your closing prayer.

Safe in His Embrace

The Last Leg of the Journey

"Do not be anxious about anything, but in everything, by prayer and petition, with thanksgiving, present your requests to God. And the peace of God, which transcends all understanding, will guard your hearts and your minds in Christ Jesus" (Phil. 4:6-7).

We have arrived at the last leg of our journey. The next two precepts in God's prescription to the prophet Samuel for His children's restoration assign responsibilities to others besides Had.

"As for me, far be it from me that I should sin against the LORD by failing to pray for you" (v. 23). I not only believe that the body of Christ shirks its duty by failing to pray for the full restoration of her Hads but I also believe Scripture implies that its sin of failing to pray is directly against God. We have a responsibility to fulfill in the process of Had's full restoration. Fervent intercessory prayer for sinners to be restored accomplishes great things.

Are people interceding for you? If so, thank them. Are you currently interceding for others or do you know people for whom you need to intercede? If so, write a prayer of intercession for them in the margin.

"I will teach you the way that is good and right" (v. 23). Had, you are in desperate need of good, solid, godly counsel. You need to know how to proceed from where you are to where God wants you to go. Your own vision, perception, and estimation have failed you. You need the help of wise others. You also need to know how and why you took a wrong way. This is an extremely important part of your knowing the way from here.

You cannot get through this process wholly restored on your own. You need members of the body of Christ, and some of them need you!

In Had situations where I've taken a primary role (always as part of a team), I have insisted on an intense time of detoxification, deprogramming, and reprogramming. I think they are critical, and I want to explain what each means.

Detoxification. The same serpent that got his fangs into Eve got his fangs into you. How he did it and what happened as a result differs. In some way, as 2 Corinthians 11:2-3 says, the serpent has corrupted and seduced your mind. Think of that corruption like a poison, venom, or toxin.

In order to detoxify, you must cut yourself off from the source or sources and all connections to the source. You may really need some stiff accountability to accomplish this detoxification, but it is vital that you do.

What in your life do you need to cut yourself off from

in order to detoxify? ______________________________

Deprogramming. Satan did a fine job of programming your mind with lies and junk that needs dumping. Every satanic stronghold involves believing a lie or lies. Seduction involves believing a very subtle arsenal of them.

For a while, you would be wise to avoid any kind of media entertainment that encourages corrupt thinking. Your mind will be very susceptible and sensitive. What might not bother the person sitting next to you could send you into a tailspin, even a possible relapse.

Consider deprogramming from all sorts of deceptive forms of media until you are fully restored. Then you can make the decision as to whether such programs even have a place in your life. All sorts of media that don't fuel temptation or compromise godly character are available to Christians. Consider carefully what goes into your mind.

Reprogramming. A Had needs to reprogram with the truth of God's Word. Get into an in-depth Bible study with a small accountability group. If you can find a Bible study that speaks directly to your needs, that's all the better! Consider maintaining an active relationship with God through His Word for the rest of your life. We can't recognize lies if we don't know truth.

What steps do you need to take for restoration or to strengthen your walk? Write them in the margin.

Isaiah 1:16-17 says, "Stop doing wrong, learn to do right!" Doing right is a learned behavior that comes from being taught. The word *disciple* means "pupil" or "learner." We will never cease to be God's children, but when we cease learning and being teachable, we are no longer disciples.

Steps with Indelible Prints

Today will be our last look at 1 Samuel 12:20-25. I pray you will apply these principles to your life as you seek restoration or grow in obedience.

"There is now no condemnation for those who are in Christ Jesus" (Rom. 8:1).

"Be sure to fear the LORD and serve him faithfully" (v. 24). The prophet Samuel's God-given prescription began with the words "Do not be afraid" (v. 20). Only one kind of fear is wise. Be sure to fear the Lord.

God is huge. He is awesome, indeed terrifying. He is powerful. He holds all the keys to life and death, ecstasy and agony. He is sovereign, and He answers to no one. He holds the oceans in the palm of His hands. The lightning checks in with Him. He is holy and does not wink at wickedness. He lifts up and He casts down. He makes the mind and can break the mind. When He rises from His throne, His enemies scatter. He has no equal. He is complete, pure, unadulterated otherness.

Read the following verses and complete the statements:

Proverbs 1:7

The fear of the LORD is ________________________________.

Proverbs 9:10

The fear of the LORD is ________________________________.

Proverbs 16:6

Through the fear of the LORD a man ________________.

God hasn't forgiven you, me, or anyone else because our sins were no big deal. He has forgiven us because of His great love. Period. He loves us so much He threw all our transgressions on His own perfect Son and let Him die on a cross in our place. We simply chose to receive the gift. We must never take lightly all that is involved in our redemption and restoration.

"Consider what great things he has done for you" (v. 24). Years ago I begged God never to let me forget what He has done for me. His mercies are new every morning. God applies them to me every single day of my needy life, but I never want to lose sight of where I've been and some of the places He's had to come to my rescue.

I pray God will continue to sustain an overwhelming gratitude in me and that He will do the same in you. The accuser says, "Feel guilty and condemned for all the great things the Most High has had to do for you." The more you listen, the more he'll say. Believe God's Word instead.

When we consider God's great deeds in a healthy, Spirit-led way, it releases a fountain of gratitude and praise. When the accuser reminds us, he poisons the waters with guilt and condemnation.

"If you persist in doing evil, both you and your king will be swept away" (v. 25). God extended complete grace and mercy to the Israelites and gave them the perfect remedy for their restoration. However, He tagged a vital warning to the end: Don't persist in doing evil.

"He who called you is faithful, and he will do it" (1 Thess. 5:24).

God entered into a blood covenant with us through Jesus Christ, and He will never leave us or forsake us. Being swept away could, however, apply to our earthly experience. It could mean swept away from usefulness, from the fellowship of the body of Christ, from His fellowship, from our giftedness, from our places of service, or even from our earthly lives. God makes no bones about His willingness in extreme cases to take His children home if that's the only way to keep them from destruction (see Acts 5).

God can work everything together for good and redeem our failures. He will gladly be strong in our weaknesses and show us His gracious favor. He can plunder the enemy and take back what Satan stole from us. But we cannot persist in doing evil.

God does not ask us for perfection. God did not say, "If you don't pull your act together and start acting perfectly, you'll be swept away." He said that if they persisted in the evil that got them into their mess, they would face serious consequences. The same is true for us.

Cast yourself on Him if you don't believe you can leave a life of sin. Ask Him to raise up an army to defend you against the enemy.

God will enable you to obey Him! Claim Philippians 4:13. Personalize it in the margin.

Your feelings of hopelessness and helplessness come straight from the enemy. They are lies. Surrender yourself to God, withholding nothing, and ask Him to do what seems impossible. Humble yourself and receive the help He will send as you seek it.

day Three

Cleaning Our Conscience

"If the Son sets you free, you will be free indeed" (John 8:36).

We can sincerely confess our sin and even turn from the sin yet still die a thousand deaths at the stab wounds of a guilty conscience. We often take God our confessions for forgiveness but not our consciences for cleansing.

If you have repented of sin and still struggle with a guilty conscience, how has that affected you?

____

We often still suffer from a guilty conscience even after sincere repentance, so what has gone wrong? The body of Christ suffers from unbelief. We do not accept and believe the full work of God's redemption.

One of the most powerful names I've ever heard given to the conscience is *recorder.* That ought to make plenty of sense to any of us who know the agony of our minds rewinding and replaying an old tape incessantly. We keep waiting for the tape to wear out, but it never does.

The Word of God equips us with at least five facts about the conscience:

1. *People with a guilty past can still enjoy a clear conscience.* The person God chose to say more about the conscience than anyone else in the Bible is the Apostle Paul. I don't know of a person in the New Testament who had more grounds for harboring guilt. He considered himself to be the least of the apostles and the chief of sinners, yet God completely purified his conscience.

2. *Good deeds cannot accomplish a clear conscience.* We can lavishly offer gifts of talents, time, money, and sacrifices, but we still won't be able to clear our consciences. Trying to earn our right to be forgiven constitutes nothing but dead works. So does attempting to make sure God never regrets forgiving and restoring us by doing good things following our failure. All we can do to secure a clean conscience is to receive the work He's already done.

3. *The Holy Spirit works with the believer's conscience.* God desires that we become spiritually healthy enough through faith to have a conscience that rightly interprets the work of the Holy Spirit. A continued guilty conscience

following sincere repentance can be the Holy Spirit's way of telling us we have not allowed or believed God to complete a desired work in us.

4. *The conscience is an indicator, not a transformer.* On its own, the conscience has no power to change us. In fact, without submitting to the authority and agreement of the Holy Spirit, it can do little more than condemn and mislead us. The Spirit of God released to dwell through the Word of God is the only One who can completely transform a defeated life.

5. *The conscience can be seared.* Something is terribly wrong if we can continue in sin and hypocrisy without a guilty conscience. Our sorrow leading to repentance is the way the Holy Spirit bears witness that we belong to God. If you don't have it, the Spirit of God may not be dwelling in you, and you may not have salvation.

If we are "in the faith" but our conscience seems to be more callous when we sin and haven't repented, we have distanced ourselves from God. If this is you, ask the Lord to show you what is wrong. Seek godly counsel and the filling of the Spirit who brings sorrow that leads to repentance.

WHEN GODLY PEOPLE DO UNGODLY THINGS

BETH MOORE

If you enjoyed these studies from Beth Moore and desire to purchase your own copy of her book *When Godly People Do Ungodly Things* to read and study in greater detail, visit the LifeWay Christian Store serving you. Or you can order a copy by calling 1-800-233-1123.

Defining a Clean Conscience

Two critical elements must be present if we're going to live day to day with the joy and relief of a clean conscience: sanctification (holiness) and sincerity.

1. *Pursue and practice the sincere and sanctified life in the world.* This means behaving consistently whether we're in the world or in the church. We only find relief when we ask God to invade our life and personality so fully that we become the same person at the shopping mall or restaurant that we are at church. Consistency is a vital component in a clean conscience.

Do people see you the same out in the world as they see you at church? ❑ Yes ❑ No ❑ I'm not sure.

2. *Pursue and practice the sanctified life in our relations with other Christians.* We play so many games at church and in our religious life! Our masquerades are so important to us that we let them talk us into choosing misery over liberty. We don't get the help we need at church because so few are willing to admit they have ever had a problem.

God will immeasurably bless your life if you are willing to get real and not act as if you've never been Had. In fact, He may grace your future with a greater harvest than your past if you're willing to be real.

A Stop at the Cross

Read and meditate on Hebrews 10:19-23. Who is the writer addressing? ______________________

"May I never boast except in the cross of our Lord Jesus Christ, through which the world has been crucified to me, and I to the world" (Gal. 6:14).

The writer addressed believers who still had need of cleansing from a guilty conscience. So, what are the biblical steps to a fresh, clean conscience?

1. *Believe what God has already done for you.* The way has been paved by the blood of Jesus. The curtain that separated us from God has been ripped from top to bottom by the tearing of the precious flesh of Jesus Christ.

2. *Go into the Holy of Holies and take your heavy conscience.* Approach God with every ounce of baggage weighing down your conscience.

How does Hebrews 4:16 tell us to approach the throne of grace? ______________________

According to this verse, what will we receive?

____

"Let us draw near to God with a sincere heart in full assurance of faith, having our hearts sprinkled to cleanse us from a guilty conscience and having our bodies washed with pure water" (Heb.10:22).

3. *Approach God with absolute sincerity and repentance.* If you realize you've never repented of the sin, repent with all your might. Pour out your heart before God. He is a refuge (Ps. 62:8). He's been waiting for you to come to Him for relief. Play the old tape for Him by telling Him what you keep hearing in your own mind, heart, or conscience. Withhold nothing.

4. *Ask God to cleanse your conscience just as His Word says.* The blood Christ shed on the cross is the means of remission for our sins. But Hebrews 10:22 says it is also the means for the complete cleansing of the consciences of those who already know Christ. *Remission* means "to send away." In remitting our sins God takes them from us and places them on the sacrificial Lamb.

Enter into a time of prayer and intimacy with God, telling Him how much you want to be free of your guilt and how desperate you are to receive a clean conscience.

5. *Approach God with a full assurance of faith.* God is more than willing to cleanse us from the guilt of repented sin! On the basis of Christ's accomplished work on Calvary, He will never turn us down as we approach Him.

For us to personally apply the accomplished work, however, we've got to believe God will do what He says He will do! Christ came for the express purpose of forgiving sin and cleansing us from all unrighteousness. He wants nothing more than to give you and me the grace gift of a fresh, clean conscience with which to enjoy our full redemption.

6. *Record this process over the old tape.* Sadly, people die with old tapes still playing in their minds and haunting their consciences. The tape is established in our memory. No amount of determination or time can make a powerful old tape cease playing in our minds and consciences.

We have to record over the old tape with the truth of God's Word and the testimony of His fresh work! I cannot take back my past sins, but I can allow God to forgive me, restore me, redeem every mistake I've made, and cleanse my guilty conscience. Thereby, through the power of the Holy Spirit, my past is reframed, and its destructive power is diffused.

Take something Satan uses to accuse you and write your new response in the margin.

7. *Where possible and appropriate, make amends or restitution.* We never want to unload our guilt at the cost of someone else's unnecessary devastation. Often, however, those we have wronged are aware of our transgression. Sometimes we don't feel released from a sin we've confessed and turned from because God desires for us to follow through by asking forgiveness or righting a wrong. Go and ask forgiveness, taking full responsibility for your sin.

Do you need to go to someone to make amends or restitution? If so, write their initials here. ___________

Do whatever it takes. It is so worth it. Christ is so worth it. He will grace you in ways you never dreamed possible.

Going Home

Thank you for sharing this journey with me. My prayer is that you will find the healing, freedom, and joy that only Christ can bring.

You might appear to others to have pulled it together. You might never fall for another seduction. You might go forward with more humility than you've ever had. You might serve with more purity of heart than you knew a mortal could have. But you will not be healed. I want to tell you why.

No book on Christian restoration would be complete without the prodigal's story. It's the most well-known, even well-loved, account of the wandering child's return to God, yet it may be the least personally experienced. Plenty of prodigals go home, but that's not enough to heal their infected wounds.

Until you let go of every other lifeline and throw yourself into it, you will remain bound, not by your seduction but by your self-punishment.

"He got up and came to his father. But while he was still a long way off, his father saw him, and felt compassion for him, and ran and embraced him, and kissed him" (Luke 15:20).

Read Luke 15:11-32. In what ways can you relate to the prodigal son? ______________________________

A true son can stay in the distance only so long until an overwhelming hunger that no one can satisfy begins to gnaw at his soul.

Do you want to go home but, like the prodigal, would you feel better about the whole thing if you just went back as a servant instead of a son? Thousands do it, but it never brings relief. They work maniacally trying to make up to God for what they've done. "I am no longer worthy to be called your son" (Luke 15:19).

They never were. They just never knew. They'd feel better if they could just take a beating like a runaway slave returned to the taskmaster. You've already had a beating!

Our penance has already been paid. Sure, you've got a lot of work to do so you can allow the Holy Spirit to sanctify you through and through. But restoration? God does that all by Himself. You just have to stand there as humbled as you've ever been in your life and come face-to-face with grace.

And how about that big brother at your Father's house? He may eye you. He may judge you. He may resent like crazy any hint that God may choose to use you. But he is not your Father, and he is not in charge.

Big brother won't mind if you come back as long as you hang your head and wear your shame. But when God has the audacity to give you a little dignity back and you dare lift your radiant face to heaven in liberated praise, big brother may be appalled!

You don't ever have to apologize that God has forgiven you and has loved you enough to accept you without question and restore you. If you surrender all you've been through to His purposes, you don't have to apologize if He uses your disaster for your good. You don't even have to apologize if He dares to use you shamelessly after what you have done.

What is God asking of us? Unabashed, unhindered, completely abandoned repentance! No faking. No hedging. No blaming. No excuses. All God wants out of us when we come home is repentance and humility.

Do not go back to your Father's table to eat the crumbs on the floor like a dog. Think more of His redemption than that. Do not go back to your Father's house just to be safe. He wants far more for you than that. You will never heal if you only go back to your Father's home. You must go back to His heart. Closer than you've ever been.

There He is now. Coming across the field. He is running in your direction. He only has eyes for you. Forget your speeches. He wants to hug you. He wants to kiss you. Let Him hold you so close that you can hear His heart pounding from having run to you.

Don't stop Him when He wants to put a robe on your back. A ring on your finger. Sandals on your feet. Do not take this moment from Him. Feast on the fatted calf. Don't be afraid! He wouldn't run like that if He weren't glad to see you! Look at the way He's springing up that hill! He's yelling something. I can't quite make it out. Oh, now I hear it. He's yelling, "Son!"

That was your name all along! Farewell, Had.

Write Micah 7:8 in the margin and claim it as your own!

I tricked you into thinking I would never be all right.
That's what I thought too. I lied.
My God thought differently, and I've decided to believe Him instead of you.
My enemy, You've been Had.

NOTES

To the Leader:

Contact prospects and those participants who have been absent lately. Encourage them to join you for your study of *What Every Christian Ought to Know* by Adrian Rogers. Better yet, visit those persons and take them a copy of the next issue of *MasterWork*.

Before the Session

1. Print Matthew 16:19 on small cards for every participant.
2. Be prepared to read the words of "Softly and Tenderly" (p. 312, *The Baptist Hymnal*, 1991).

During the Session

1. Ask: *When you're returning home after a long journey, do the last few hours fly or creep by? Do you stop for the night or push your way on home? Why?* OR Ask two volunteers of the same sex to stand and hug one another. Ask: *Why is a hug nice? How can a hug make someone feel safe?* FOR EITHER OPTION Explain that returning home after being seduced away from God is a long journey, but believers must keep pushing until they make it all the way home. They can be assured the Father will wrap them in His safe, loving embrace when they arrive.
2. Share with learners: *Last week we studied several prescriptions for restoration from 1 Samuel 12:20-25. The first two precepts we'll look at today lay a responsibility on other believers to help fallen believers make their way home.* Request that someone read 1 Samuel 12:20-25 to review. Ask how we can sin against God, according to verse 23. Distribute the Matthew 16:19 cards. Ask participants to form small groups and pray that Satan will be bound and the Spirit loosed in each person's life. Encourage participants to write the names of those in their group on their cards as a reminder to pray for them throughout this week.
3. Ask why seduced believers need the body of Christ in order to learn the way that is right and good. Ask the class to identify the three critical, yet radical, steps to learning what is right and good (p. 158). Discuss some specific examples of detoxification. Explain that deprogramming literally means to cut off media programs that reinforce seduction. Ask: *How can media, even a sitcom or commercial, prevent the full restoration of someone who's been seduced?* Invite someone to read Matthew 12:43-45. Ask: *What's the danger of detoxifying and deprogramming without reprogramming? What must we put into our lives in place of whatever seduced us?* Ask participants to read Psalm 19:10 and name truths about

NOTES

God's Word. Invite volunteers to share how God's Word has protected them with its wise warnings.

4. Discuss the first activity of Day 2 (p. 159). Inquire: *How can fearing the Lord pull you out of Satan's seductions? How can reviewing the great things God has done for you form a wall of protection around your soul? How can you use Romans 8:1 against Satan when he tries to condemn you for past actions?* Ask participants to share the warning God gave His people at the end of His prescription in 1 Samuel 12. Ask what they think it means to be swept away. Request that participants regroup with the people they prayed with earlier. Direct them to use Philippians 4:13 and 1 Thessalonians 5:24 to form a response to a seduced believer who declares he or she simply cannot quit doing evil. Allow groups to share.
5. Ask: *What one word would you use to describe living with a guilty conscience?* Invite participants to share their responses to the first activity in Day 3 (p. 161) without getting too personal. Ask why they think believers still suffer from a guilty conscience even after sincere repentance. Ask participants to list five facts about the conscience. Reinforce those facts by reading Romans 9:1-2; 1 Corinthians 4:3-4; Hebrews 9:9; and 1 Timothy 4:2. Explore the meaning of a seared conscience. Ask participants to read 2 Corinthians 1:12 and share how Paul described a clean conscience. Discuss the two critical elements necessary for a clean conscience. Use the activities and text in Day 4 to discuss the biblical steps to a clean conscience.
6. As you read Luke 15:11-32, urge participants to listen as if they have never heard the story before. Ask: *In what ways does this prodigal son resemble a believer who's been Had? What's the difference between coming home as a servant and as a son? Why will we never heal if we only go back to our Father's home? What does it mean to go back to His heart? How can we get there? What will our Father do when we get there?* Read "Softly and Tenderly" as your closing prayer.